MU00776902

With a provocative premise, in: style, Harvey's book is an all-har tanic strategy to corrupt our ch. joke to some, but any Christian who reads this book will discover that it's no laughing matter to God.

—ED VITAGLIANO, *news editor for the American Family Association Journal and minister for twenty-five years*

♦   ♦   ♦

Linda Harvey has sounded the alarm for parents and anyone else who will listen: Our kids are embracing the darkness and the impact on their spiritual lives is disastrous. *Not My Child: Contemporary Paganism and New Spirituality* is a must read for those not willing to turn our children over to paganism.

—CARMEN PATE, *Cohost, Point of View Radio Talk Show*

♦   ♦   ♦

If you want to maintain a false sense of down-home, All-American, optimistic tranquility, DO NOT BUY THIS BOOK! If you do, you will *not* put it down, and you will *not* get its warnings out of your head. Linda Harvey writes both with great intelligence and down-to-earth vivid readability showing how pagan chicken soup for the soul is being served up in massive doses to our rising generations of unsuspecting kids, while most parents look on in blissful ignorance. If you want to understand how modern culture is being profoundly undermined by an ideology as old as the hills but made to look like the latest slick video game, YOU MUST BUY THIS BOOK!

—PETER JONES, PHD, *Director, Christian Witness to a Pagan Planet, Scholar-in-Residence and Adjunct Professor, Westminster in California*

The mysterious has captivated children from the time of fairy tales, but the new wrinkle of paganism and feminist spirituality is more than innocent scares and the thrill of creative imagination. The indoctrination inherent in today's "spirituality" is supplanting a biblical worldview and undermining Judeo-Christian beliefs and values. This campaign is detailed in Linda Harvey's book—*Not My Child: Contemporary Paganism and New Spirituality*. It is must reading for every concerned parent!

> —JANICE SHAW CROUSE, PHD, *an official U.S. delegate to the UN children's summit and authority on feminist spirituality. Director and Senior Fellow, The Beverly LaHaye Institute, Concerned Women for America*

◆　◆　◆

Linda Harvey's *Not My Child* warns us that kids without the built-in "nonsense detector" of traditional faith are being seduced by a thriving occult, often through the Internet. When Christianity leaves the scene or becomes lukewarm, there is no neutral zone. Witches, warlocks and other spiritual counterfeits quickly move in to slake the God-given thirst for meaning beyond the material present. And they often bring a sexual agenda with them. In this well-written book, Mrs. Harvey rips the lid off this profoundly dangerous pagan trend and tells what parents need to do to protect their kids.

> —ROBERT KNIGHT, *director of Culture and Media Institute, a division of the Media Research Center*

◆　◆　◆

Linda Harvey's book is a must read for every parent and grandparent in America. She has done the research, investigation and analysis that is so desperately needed—in exposing the paganism that is infiltrating our educational system and entertainment industry. Buy this book, read it and pass it on to another parent!

> —BOB BURNEY, *Host—Bob Burney Live! WRFD Radio, Columbus, Ohio*

not my child

Contemporary Paganism & the New Spirituality

Linda Harvey

not my child

Contemporary Paganism & the New Spirituality

An Imprint of AMG Publishers.

Not My Child: Contemporary Paganism and New Spirituality
Copyright © 2008 by Linda Harvey
Published by Living Ink Books, an imprint of AMG Publishers
6815 Shallowford Rd.
Chattanooga, Tennessee 37421

Published in association with the literary agency of The Loyal Arts Literary Agency, PO Box 1414, Bend, Oregon 97709.

ISBN 978-089957034-1

First printing—January 2008
Cover designed by Left Coast Graphics, Portland, Oregon
Interior design and typesetting by Sans Serif, Inc., Saline, Michigan
Edited and Proofread by Michele Huey, Dan Penwell, Sharon Neal, and Rick Steele

Printed in the United States of America
13 12 11 10 09 08 –CH– 7 6 5 4 3 2 1

Library of Congress Cataloging-in-Publication Data

Harvey, Linda, 1950-
  Not my child : contemporary paganism and new spirituality / Linda Harvey.
     p. cm.
  ISBN 978-0-89957-034-1 (pbk. : alk. paper)
  1. Occultism--Religious aspects--Christianity. 2. Neopaganism--Controversial literature. 3. Teenagers--Religious life. 4. Parent and teenager--Religious aspects--Christianity. I. Title.
  BR115.O3H37 2008
  261.2'994--dc22
                          2007049790

Dedicated to and in memory of
Alene Bailey Myers
1922–2007

The best mom a girl could ever have.

Acknowledgments

This book has been a long time in the making. There are so many people to thank, starting first of all with Dan Penwell and all the folks at AMG who saw the project and believed in it, and Matt Jacobson, who wisely steered me around unforeseen obstacles. The great editing of Michele Huey and the proofreading of Sharon Neal—these ladies provided many improvements to the original.

I want to also thank the early comments and edits done by my thoughtful daughter, Sarah, and my dear friend Diane Cartalano, who took valuable time away from parenting and other life stresses to give me solid input.

I'm eternally grateful to all the friends and co-laborers in culture battles who have prayed for me and for Mission America over the years. And most of all, I thank my family and my precious husband, Tom, who not only gave wonderful feedback but also streamlined home life during critical periods. He never gave up praying, and still hasn't.

CONTENTS

The Faith That Now Dares to Speak Its Name

"Suddenly, Kate was looking at the Come to Me Love Spell differently. Could she really do it? Could she make Scott Coogan notice her, even fall in love with her, just by doing a spell in a book? . . . *But what have you got to lose?* the voice in her head asked." (*Circle of Three: So Mote It Be*, 22–23)

It seemed harmless to my friend and me—a wooden board painted with the alphabet and numbers. It had been around for decades, and I had never met anyone, my parents included, who believed there was a problem.

In the 1890s a man named William Fuld introduced a novelty called the Ouija board into the recreational world of America. Parker Brothers picked it up for mass production in the 1960s, and soon several million units were in the hands of American kids—like me at age fourteen.

Anne and I giggled as we read the directions.

"What makes this thing move?" I asked.

We decided it must be our nerve endings, but each of us secretly believed the other one was pushing the little pointer used to highlight the numbers and letters. But as we asked it questions, each resting our fingertips lightly on one side, the little plastic device raced along, spelling out answers. Often the response was gibberish, but sometimes it wasn't. It told me, in answer to the question on every girl's mind, that I was going to marry a guy named Phil. I never married a Phil.

> "Gena threw an M&M in the air and caught it in her mouth. 'I guess this meeting of the Fortunetellers Club has officially begun.' Anne dug through her divination tools and pulled out the deck of fortune-telling cards she'd bought the last time she'd been to the Village"
> (*The Ghost of Shady Lane*, 31).

Anne and I soon put the board away and went on to other teen girl interests. Yet this episode remained at the hazy edge of memory, unexplained until I became a Christian as an adult.

The traditions of my faith provided clear instruction about this sort of thing, but my teenage mind had danced past it. It wasn't as if I had no exposure to the gospel message. With worship services, Sunday school, vacation Bible school, and confirmation classes, I spent a lot of time at our Episcopal church. But never to my recollection were we warned about certain practices like divination (fortune-telling) that are called "abominations" in Deuteronomy 18. In fact, a serious adherence to Scripture would have been way too fundamentalist and anti-intellectual in the Anglican faith climate.

So there was no reason to hesitate when, in my later teens and in college, I became fascinated by what is called "parapsychology." I read about experiments at Duke University and other institutions, about Edgar Cayce, past lives, and reincarnation.

As a young adult, I faithfully followed my horoscope and even bought tarot cards, although they were soon collecting dust in the back of a drawer. By God's grace, I never worshipped a goddess or tried to make contact with any "spirits." I found the star charts and card-reading too silly, overly complicated, and off-base to bring real meaning into my busy secular life. So I, like most of my generation, slithered out of sorcery's grasp.

Looking back, I realize the decades of my adolescence were transitional ones, where an America in flux nevertheless retained a national ethic steeped in biblical mores. Those of us raised in the fifties, sixties, and seventies still benefit from immunities obtained then. Marriage, respect for God, virginity, honesty—all were the cultural norms, and even those with flimsy faith got a free ride on the coattails of the Holy Spirit. Sure, a few of my counterculture peers dove headfirst into the Age of Aquarius, with its meditation, trances, and star-charting. Still, the overall numbers of converts remained relatively small.

With our kids today, however, that is rapidly changing.

Today's American child is a product of casual spirituality, the separation of church and state, the absence of prayer in school, and the promotion of abortion and gay rights. In their world, it's going out on a limb just to say "God bless America." So is it any wonder that so many are falling under the spell of the "ancient ways"?

Resistance will be only as strong as each child's nonsense detector. Our self-indulged offspring are learning that they can and should construct designer gods to be what they need. They presume the supernatural is benevolent and ready to affirm one's self-esteem, so they exclude the notion of spiritual evil as absurd and primitive.

Their amorphous deities can be manipulated at will to become one's untapped mental abilities, a creative muse, an Amazon goddess, or a lover of Dionysian pleasures. Frequently these new gods are dressed in Christian garb with an altered "Jesus" who is no longer a savior, but can morph into a sentimental sap or a receiver of self-focused prayer as needed—or conveniently vanish in the light of the world's temptations, freeing one to partake as guiltlessly as necessary. These squishy spiritual beliefs allow the *self* to be the real boss.

But no firm foundation can be laid with Jello, and many wonder if this is a spirituality that has "a form of godliness but denying its power" (2 Tim. 3:5). Without the omnipotent power of the Holy Spirit, who is one with our Savior, Jesus Christ, malevolent spiritual forces are free to step in. So the faith that for several thousand years of history dared not speak its name in the Western world, does so boldly now.

Essentially, it is paganism.

Nature-based ritual and sorcery are being offered on the all-you-can-eat American buffet to children of all ages, and parents stand by, smiling indulgently. This is creative nourishment for our young, some believe, part of developing the "imagination" and "higher order thinking." It's "empowerment" for girls to overcome oppressive, patriarchal Western tradition. Since it's everywhere—from television to video games to science fiction to Barbie dolls to Scooby Doo cartoons—it must be all right. With hardly an eyeblink, parents giggle right along with kids and stand in line all night for the latest Harry Potter book in order to hand their children a tale that depicts modern-day children in a *school for witchcraft*. Why doesn't this ring a bell of warning somewhere? How desensitized have we become?

The world hasn't ended as our offspring explore these new spiritual journeys. Most of us continue on with life as usual. So those who urge caution are all wet—right? God is very gracious. So, life as we know it hasn't drowned in a flood of destruction—yet. Or has it?

What's behind the rash of behavioral problems American children now experience? Childhood depression, hyperactivity, panic attacks, eating disorders, suicide, substance abuse, gender identity disorders, violent child criminals, early sexual experimentation, teen pregnancies, abortions, rage against authority—the list goes on. American children are the most privileged ever in the history of humanity, yet terribly troubled. Could some of these issues result from dining on the daily bread of spiritual confusion?

Because parents have opened the gates of hell for them to peek into, believing it's the Garden of Eden, children are learning to welcome and embrace the darkness. Why do parents not realize this will have drastic implications for their spiritual lives?

God has given us so much, and yet the culture thumbs its nose at Him, bowing down instead to the goddess of American pop culture. Our overindulged offspring are spiritually starving. Can't we offer them something besides the empty plate of sorcery?

CHAPTER 1

Laying the Foundation to Build Young Pagans

"I am a sixteen-year-old high school junior, and I am a natural Wiccan. This is the religion chosen for me by my parents on the day of my birth. I am also a bisexual, and am open with such a fact each day in my Catholic high school." (E-mail message to author)

How many of you sense that there's something really wrong with our culture, our churches—and especially with our kids?

Let's say you're a parent whose son has been acting a little odd lately. You don't usually worry much about what's going on in his life, but he's thirteen, and you wonder if there's something you've missed.

So you go to his room and pick up a couple of his favorite novels. He's a big fan of Jonathan Stroud, author of *The Golem's Eye* and *Ptolemy's Gate*.

> *"Train up a child in the way he should go, and when he is old he will not depart from it"* (Prov. 22:6).

You immerse yourself in an imaginary London where the government's Department of Internal Affairs professionally employs fourteen-year-old Jonathan as a magician. His days are full of conjuring up one favorite "genie" and dealing with other assorted demons. In this world, sorcery is part of everyday life. Jonathan is also pursuing members of an underground resistance group. This is quite a plateful for a young teen who resides with an unrelated adult woman who's his boss/mentor.

This bothers you a bit, although might you tell yourself, *it's creative, and it's only fantasy.* But then, because of computer games, favorite television shows, movies, and PlayStation®, much of your son's play life involves fighting demons, seeing into the future, and discovering special "powers" (like Harry Potter had). It's frequently a *search inside oneself*, with help from any handy spirit helpers or spells.

You move on to another of your son's favorite writers. He's become captivated by Philip Pullman's tales: *The Golden Compass, The Subtle Knife,* and *The Amber Spyglass* (Scholastic, 1995, 1997, 2000). He also raved about the movie, *The Golden Compass,* which he saw with friends. But an afternoon spent in these pages leaves you shaking in your shoes.

Pullman has constructed a trilogy where multiple worlds exist simultaneously, some like ours, some carved out of a Jurassic wilderness. Witches and angels abound—but the witches are mostly good, and the angels are conflicted. In one world, every person is accompanied at all times by an animal "familiar," called a "daemon," that has strong spiritual ties to its human.

In *The Amber Spyglass*, a great secret is revealed: that Almighty God is really a fraud. He was never our Creator. He has retreated into a clouded mountain and has turned all power over to the chief angel, a ruthless Satan-figure, now head of the "Church."

And you wonder why your son is getting moody.

Yes, this is seriously troubling. Is this fantasy—or a tutorial in sorcery mixed with revolution? I firmly believe the balance has tipped over to the latter. Our children now spend an enormous amount of time in a twilight land of enchantment, where fun can quickly become a nightmare, and their curiosity morphs into obsession. We're not in Kansas anymore.

The last seconds of a countdown are ticking away before an explosion of radical pagan practices occurs among American children, yet many parents seem oblivious or only mildly concerned. The spiritual stakes for Christians are substantial. Our churches and families must decide whether we believe Scripture when it describes a bona fide evil intelligence as our "adversary," walking about as a "roaring lion, seeking whom he may devour" (1 Pet. 5:8). Is this just a powerful myth by ancients who didn't understand psychology? Or is truth playing out before our eyes precisely as it would if the demonic world really exists, just as the Bible describes?

I will explain more thoroughly in chapter 3 that my position is that the demonic realm is a reality, with paganism as one of its satellites. That may not be an easy sell in today's America, but I hope to provide a clear explanation about how my own worldview changed from that of a scoffer to one who accepts the reality of supernatural evil. I believe this because I accept God's Word as true. I also believe that these spiritual tactics are becoming increasingly predictable and observable. There's no witch hunt here because paganism is everywhere.

Can people believe these things without getting all spooky and seeing visions or having out-of-body experiences? Yes. We can approach this rationally, knowing that the Almighty God of the universe is supreme, always contending on behalf of our families, as we continue to trust and rely on Him.

If the gospel is accurate, it has enormous implications as we observe the deterioration of our culture. Enemy battalions surround the American home, while we carry on, mostly unaware of the coming assault. But *why* is this happening now? Why (apparently) didn't our parents and grandparents have to deal with such an onslaught? Are Christian parents the only ones who find reason for concern? And what can we do about it?

The Framework of Today's Paganism

Paganism, witchcraft, and sorcery involve a number of practices by which practitioners seek to contact supernatural forces and use them for their own purposes. And most importantly, these spiritual forces—whether through ignorance or deliberate rebellion—are *not* the Christian God of the Bible. We will go more deeply into a description in chapter 2.

Some observers call it the fastest-growing religion in America. The number of adherents is difficult to determine, but estimates are that over 1.5 million pagans and witches exist in America, and the number is rising each year.[1] And this is just an estimate of adults. Today's primary growth is among youth.

It's not simply an American phenomenon. Dr. Peter Jones, author of the best-selling book *Cracking Da Vinci's Code* (Victor Books, 2004), is a native of Great Britain, resides in California, and regularly travels throughout the globe. He says that although witchcraft is the fastest-growing religion in Britain and Australia, paganism is most powerful in America. Our Christian population notwithstanding, this country is the "incubator" for neopaganism. It is "going global," but it was born in the USA.[2]

Several broad cultural changes have facilitated the pagan incursion among youth, such as the following:

- The empowerment of youth outside the bounds of the family
- The decline of respect for biblical Christianity
- An intense focus on nature and environmentalism
- "Human rights" agendas that overturn tradition, particularly feminism, homosexual rights, and cross-gender activism
- Popularity among youth of intense anti-Americanism
- Renewed interest in alternative religious practices—even in so-called Christian churches

These aren't solo influences but rather interlocking choruses making strident, incessant noise impossible to tune out.

Dissing the Past

How is the soil prepared for the new spirituality? First, clear the fields and that means sweeping away all that has gone before.

- Christianity has to go.
- American patriotism, out of here.
- Male leadership, forget it.
- Traditional methods of parenting and instruction, hit the road.

Children are hearing that they deserve the freedom to roam malls and libraries, cruise the Web, even determine their own health care. Yet what they are urged to explore is not mathematics, science, or classical literature, but trashy pulp paperbacks, psychic hot lines, and sex-change surgery. Girls are spoon-fed a simmering stew of rage against masculinity mixed with sensual indulgence, vanity, and occult spirituality. Boys are castigated for being male and having too much aggression, then handed tools of supernatural "empowerment" through fantasy and role-playing games.

At the same time, our culture is dismissing—or irrationally re-vamping—our traditional Judeo-Christian heritage. Knee-jerk epi-thets about so-called inconsistencies in the Bible are memorized now by high schoolers in order to deal with "pushy" (i.e., committed) Christians who want to express their beliefs openly. Faithful young believers try to stand up to anti-Christian bigotry, as well as depraved behavior among their peers. But this generation is immersed in wholesale rebellion involving cheating, drugs, binge drinking, pornography, and oral sex parties. These interlocking circles of defi-ance produce an incoherent self-indulgence often wrapped around a dark faith.

Meanwhile parents struggle to cope with this social implosion, most without realizing that something worse is coming or, in some cases, is already here. It's one thing to deal with a daughter who hates males but will debate with you about the issue; it's quite another to deal with a child who is hearing voices telling her to do something violent about the male "problem."

To make matters worse, new educational and parenting philosophies, along with weak Christian role models, have created an impression among youth that they can and should leave the past behind, that the old ways have no convincing truths, and new "progressive" ideas about social roles, as well as spirituality, are superior. With few adequate defenses of past heritage, they see simple solutions:

- More women in charge
- More respect for Hindus, Buddhists, Muslims
- Fewer remnants of Western culture (which, of course, is responsible for the vast evil in the world—as children have been taught)

Diversity and multiculturalism dominate elementary and middle school social studies curricula, as well as high school literature required reading lists. Yet the themes are less often about racial, religious, or cultural harmony, and more about acceptance of any idea or behavior, no matter how bizarre, high-risk, or downright phony. *The unique and outlandish is in.* One must have *no* committed beliefs at all, lest one be too exclusive or even "hateful." This unjustly isolates and depicts biblically faithful Christians as being backward, intolerant, even inhumane.

In fact, the all-pervasive, anti-bias curricula today generally have a three-pronged focus: *teaching tolerance on the basis of race, religion, and sexual orientation.* But often, the new "tolerance" actually foments more divisiveness. The religious component of many of these programs present garbled messages that leave kids with the impression that fervent Christian faith equals rabid racism.

Educating for Rebellion

One middle school "tolerance" curriculum is called *Healing the Hate*, published through a grant by the U.S. Department of Justice. It presents an in-depth lesson describing the experience of "Floyd," a young man who joined the Aryan Nation white supremacist group. Floyd talks about his background: "As a youth, I had gone to Baptist, Pentecostal, and other churches. . . . I became fascinated with history and the story of Adolf Hitler." After he joined the group, he attended Sunday morning worship services and Bible studies on Wednesday night. The young man describes the group's racist and violent activities, but, after a time, he became troubled by certain things. "I started asking questions about their teachings of the Bible. Whenever I asked a question they couldn't answer, they told me to shut up—that I asked too many questions." He eventually left the group.[3]

To today's casually religious preteen, this lesson is likely to produce the inaccurate association that all Christians who read and study their Bibles are ignorant, potentially violent neo-Nazis. And one can't help but believe this was the lesson's intent. Such anti-Christian themes at school are becoming bolder and more acceptable. As a result, whatever instruction given at Sunday school is virtually wiped out on Monday, and kids flounder in a sea of ideological uncertainty. Most parents have no clue about the poison that's slowly killing their child's faith.

Once they walk through the schoolhouse door, children are their own authorities in some of the most serious areas of life. Self-determination for minors is now standard practice in areas such as health care, sexuality, and sources of information—and this shift in responsibility is occurring rapidly. Girls have abortions at age thirteen without parental consent. On-site wellness centers in high schools assure confidentiality, often excluding parents as they send Jake or Katie to Planned Parenthood, the local homosexual youth center, or to the public library to research alternative religions. On the pretext of "stress reduction," private mental health counseling can undermine parental mores, as well as faith, without parental notification.

Many observers of U.S. schools have detailed the influence of radical educational philosophies on the academic training of today's American child. Broadly speaking, the past is up for *revision* or *exclusion* based on new, more enlightened viewpoints. Heritage no longer matters if it gets in one's way. Children have become empowered "learners," and teachers are now dethroned "facilitators" of learning.

To bring it to a very practical spiritual application, the circle that is cast in witchcraft covens perfectly illustrates this idea. No one is in charge. All are equal, people as well as ideas. There is no hierarchy or leadership, no distinction between better or worse beliefs, and, like all circles, it ultimately goes nowhere, with self at the center. History, too, is being portrayed as an endless repetition of cycles (reminiscent of Elton John's song, "The Circle of Life" from *The Lion King*). Today's humans are only bit players on a much larger stage that includes plant and animal life (equal to human life, according to environmental "science"), past human lives, revered ancient cultures (such as the pre-Christian "matriarchies" believed to have existed in Europe), and folktales, mythology, and personal stories and journals, elevated above actual historical fact.

All of this is part of the exaltation of the individual and the ethic of selfhood. Rather than seeing people as connected necessarily to biological families, a new paradigm insists that experience and perceptions of the individual matter above all else, and that each is perfectly capable of forming his/her own goals, values, and direction. This new isolated person should be allowed to function autonomously from childhood. Consequently, the worth of the past is diminished, along with the need for pesky interference from parents who might question the enthroning of "me" in the life of the child.

Traditional mental health principles reveal that most personality disorders result from too intense a focus on "self." And that's exactly what Christianity has taught all along, only it's called by another name—sin.

The Sacrificial Altar of Global Human Rights

Where do such ideas get started? Besides the Garden of Eden, some originate at the grassroots and move up. Simultaneously there's a "top-down" ideology and current examples of rebellion in high places. One influential expression of such new, radical ideas about youth is the proposed Declaration of the Rights of the Child.[4] Drafted by the United Nations in 1989, it is a radical reworking of the document of the same name that was first adopted in 1959. Member nations have been asked to ratify the new version, and only the United States has not done so.

While this document contains some valuable provisions that would serve to protect children, it also frames in the name of "human rights" new freedoms that would put children in harm's way by emancipating them from parental oversight. Provisions that are more radical overshadow the positives—such as guarantees of food, clothing, shelter, etc. It is important to note that the global vision of human rights now insists that all faiths, sexual orientations/behavior, and cultural traditions be accepted and celebrated. Opposition or exclusive beliefs are considered to be discriminatory.

One proposal in this treaty is that children should have access to all sources of "information." The influential American Library Association (ALA) agrees. Its position is that censorship—not government bans on material, but adults and local communities using discretion about selecting material for children—is to be resisted at all costs in libraries. It's an unwavering standard taught to librarians-in-training at universities throughout America, but becomes problematic as publishers, marketers, and pornographers exploit the natural curiosity of children as never before.

The reflection of certain provisions of the children's rights treaty within the "soft" sectors of American culture has proceeded (as with the ALA, mentioned above) despite the lack of ratification by the U.S. Senate. From teacher-training programs to universities to the media to community groups to Chambers of Commerce, through foundations, conferences, publications, and children's television shows, this freedom-of-information idea is virtually everywhere.

Any suggested limits to what children read and view is greeted by an astonished gasp and knee-jerk accusations of censorship. The brainwashing has been thorough, and our children are paying for it.

Internet screening software in libraries has been staunchly opposed by the ALA as a violation of this supposed "right" to all information. In other words, pornography, instructions on bomb-making, or—pertinent to this book—how to practice sorcery to put a curse on another student should be available to every child as a good and positive thing. Children should be allowed to make their own decisions about the worth of any message, so the thinking goes.

The declaration also maintains that a child has the right to "freedom of association." Does this mean that eight-year-old Kyle should be able to have as his best friend, without parental objections, the seventeen-year-old suspected drug dealer who lives down the street? Or how about a forty-year-old transsexual member of a coven? Increasingly, as children learn creative ways to bypass parental authority, such incidents are happening more and more on both the material and spiritual planes.

And children are being educated directly about this new standard. UNICEF has taken the children's rights declaration and made cartoons about its provisions that have been shown as public service announcements to an estimated worldwide audience of one billion, including the children's audience in the United States. Funds provided by the Cartoon Network gave a boost to this effort. So kids themselves are seeing animated lessons about the right to be protected from exploitative child labor practices (a good thing), but a different one explains a child's right to "meet and share views with others." Another cartoon tells children they have the "right to freedom of conscience."

This ideology has been adopted by a number of powerful non-profit organizations. On the subject of graphic sexual material, National Coalition Against Censorship holds the position that "there is no evidence whatsoever that minors would be harmed by seeing sexually explicit expression."[5] While most thinking parents would strongly disagree, the NCAC-supporting organizations include the National Education Association, the American Federation of Teachers, the Modern Language Association, the National Council of Teachers of English, the ACLU, and the Children's Literature Association.[6]

Books for youth advocating witchcraft or sorcery also provide creative ways to avoid parental scrutiny. In *Wild Girls: The Path of the*

Young Goddess, author Patricia Monaghan advises girls to keep a secret "spiritual" diary and "do not share it with anyone" (146). This is important, she emphasizes, because "you need space and privacy to develop a spiritual practice" (146). Since she has already described specific spells, as well as sexual "initiation" ceremonies (128) for girl readers, who may be as young as ten (xv), this may be of concern to parents whose daughter can obtain this book in any major chain or used bookstore.

Those acting in loco parentis, such as schools, often support broad decision-making freedom for children as well. Many schools have set up mechanisms for children to act without parental permission. The children's rights treaty states that no child should be "deprived of his or her right of access" to "health care services."[7] The catchall phrase, "family planning and education services," facilitates access by middle and high school students to local clinics where no parental permission is required for contraceptives or even abortions. Schools also readily provide students with contact information for local homosexual community groups, often located at a church and funded with United Way support, where "questioning" youth can explore sexuality with peers or older homosexuals. No parental notification or permission is required in most cases for kids as young as twelve or thirteen. Yet the curious adolescent doesn't usually need to go outside the school building, since over 3,600 "gay/straight alliances" (homosexual clubs) now operate in American middle and high schools.

Even those adolescents who don't utilize such services know about them and are becoming accustomed to the availability of such life-altering options without the guidance and wisdom of the adults who care about them most—their parents. So why wouldn't today's child naturally believe it's his or her business—and nobody else's— if they decide to dabble in private pagan rituals with friends? If parents don't go along with the need to "explore" questionable spiritual alternatives, the savvy child can seek out a social worker or psychologist and complain about the repressive religious climate at home.

One more aspect of tearing down the past needs to be identified, and it's evident especially among high school and college students during recent elections. There is a frenzied movement now to viciously *undermine American patriotism* among youth. Why does this matter? America-bashing is one more way our kids are being prepared for ideological alternatives. It's true not everything about our country, past or present, is defensible. But when educators, pop icons, and others our kids emulate go out of their way to declare loyalty to America's sworn enemies, or support radically anti-American elements, or even advocate outright anarchy, get ready. This creates one more vulnerable spot in the heart and mind of a student. America's spiritual, Christian heritage has value and develops discernment in the young person. The student without this foundation will believe just about anything.

The Dark Side of Entertainment

When we allow kids total freedom to explore the media world of today, all hell, literally, can break loose. The Internet greatly reduces the ability of parents to monitor a child's spiritual (and other) influences. Here's how quickly kids can get off into strange territory.

At school, a fourth grade class may read a book about "native American spirituality" as part of multicultural education. They'll read about dreamcatchers, worshipping "Raven" and "Bear," and the revered status of medicine men. Your curious child then decides to search for more information on the Internet. Quickly he may learn about current practices among Native Americans, which is likely to involve nature-based rituals and shamanism.

Or let's say your daughter's eighth grade class is studying the Salem witch trials. As she decides to look up material for a school report, guess what pops up? Spells, real Wiccans, and more.

There's a great deal of misinformation in cyberspace ready to deceive and manipulate impressionable youth. Besides the mindless and violent games, graphic pornography, and chat rooms with shady new "friends," the Internet is cited by youth themselves as the primary means of accessing more information on pagan alternatives, with many finding the tools to dabble in mysticism before parents even know. This will be explored in depth in chapter 4, but suffice to say the Web sites on witchcraft and paganism are almost infinite in number. Simply type the words "pagan," "Wicca," "spells" with the terms "teen" or "youth" into a search engine and prepare to be overwhelmed with the number of resources that arise.

"I spent an astonishing amount of time on my aunt's Internet, filling my mind with all things pagan," writes Anastasia, a sixteen-year-old witch, on www.witchvox.com. Some of the most popular pagan sites are www.teenwitch.com, with a whole array of spells for every occasion; www.mywitchshop.com; and the pagan teen pages of www.beliefnet.com.

Another nest of sites pops up around the characters of favorite fantasy books, Harry Potter being the leader. Even more arise in the murky world of online games and children's cartoons, such as World of Warcraft, Pokemon, Yu-Gi-Oh!, Sailor Moon, Hellboy, and others. The genre of "anime" is suffused with sorcery as a core activity.

The nurturing parent wants to encourage a child's curiosity, so it's hard to deny Internet exploration, especially when there is good material out there. But a *lot* more discernment is needed than many parents have been providing, in this as well as another area—youth literature.

For today's child, one of the major entry points into paganism is through novels. A study in 2002 by the Barna research group for WisdomWorks Ministries revealed that 86 percent of teens see supernatural-themed television shows or movies on a routine basis. The study also revealed that those who had read Harry Potter books or saw the movies were more liable to be interested in witchcraft and to have dabbled in occult activities.[8]

Harry Potter is old news by now. To follow up, a whole new crop of authors is churning out tons of similar, even bolder children's literature in the "fantasy" genre. People think, "the world hasn't ended, has it?" But the effects are incremental. People won't know the impact until their current children become young adults, and then it will be all new territory. We've never raised a generation immersed in these specific influences before.

You may recall, as I do, reading the Nancy Drew series or Hardy Boys when you were eleven, twelve, or thirteen. A decade ago, girls were reading the Babysitters Club and the Sweet Valley High series. Today's boy or girl who goes to the corner bookstore will find no shortage of paperback series about "growing up"—only now they also incorporate occult practices and themes, sometimes quite shocking. Spell-casting, divination, contacting the dead, seeking animal spirits—all are routine stuff in both teen pulp fiction and in the more acclaimed titles. After years of watching *Buffy, Sabrina, Charmed,* and *Medium,* this is what they expect. Channelers such as Sylvia Browne appear regularly on afternoon talk shows. Parents and kids alike have become desensitized.

The categories of fantasy and science fiction are wildly popular among preteens and teens, as are the "manga" graphic novels, which have taken off as a result of the influence of Japanese "anime" cartoons popular on Saturday morning and after-school television. In all these categories, the level of occult practices used in story lines has ratcheted up enormously in recent years. More specifics about young adult literature will be covered in chapter 4, but in a general sense, it isn't this book's purpose to recommend keeping kids away from all fantasy/science fiction and other imaginative material. But a *lot* more monitoring is needed because there are some real dangers out there, simply because of the domination of these themes. Where can kids go to read just about pets and sports anymore?

Younger and younger children are being introduced to the occult as well. There are even dolls now to satisfy the interest in spiritualism. "Secret Spells" Barbie is, like all of Mattel's popular Barbie line, marketed to children ages three and up. And the newer Bratz dolls have a whole line called Genie Magic dolls. Disney jumped on the bandwagon several years ago by issuing a book series aimed at preteen girls entitled *W.I.T.C.H.* The books feature girls who discover they possess secret magical powers and learn to use them as they seek friendships, fret over boys, or study for a test.

But again, the American Library Association and most American public schools maintain that children themselves need to be the judge of what is valid and what is not. This fits with the trend toward rewriting history and discarding heritage. Today's culture is advanced and progressive, they are told, and "new" ways of relating and behaving socially, sexually, and, now, spiritually are a great improvement over the past. Of course, as we will explore in chapter 2, there is nothing new under the sun in shamanism, spirit contact, or witchcraft.

What's new is that Americans are buying the lie that these practices are harmless fun or possibly even beneficial.

Taking Christ out of Christianity

Reinforcing the idea that the past and parents must be left behind is the growing disenchantment with and even outright antagonism toward traditional Christianity. We've already mentioned that this attitude prevails throughout the public school system, but amazingly, this approach dominates some Christian circles as well, and our youth are listening.

Two decades ago, a fledgling movement called "feminist spirituality" grew in intellectual circles and on university campuses, championed by feminists primarily from mainline Christian denominations who were taking "consciousness raising" to a new level. The movement sought to discard biblical standards of sin and atonement, as well as God the Father, in favor of a feminized deity with Eastern, pagan, and Native American religious elements. Many adherents remained in their congregations with the goal of revolution from the inside out, and have subsequently introduced feminist theology and its heresy into "Christian" churches.

When I attended a seminary of the Evangelical Lutheran Church in America in 1993, I had to sign an agreement to adhere to a policy of "inclusive language." I didn't realize this would mean that other students and I would be chastised in class if we referred to God as "He." I was stunned the first time this happened to me. This oppressive climate of political correctness has become common in mainline Christianity, shutting out the true light of authentic faith.

So your daughter Kristin, who attends youth group at one of the local mainline churches, may hear things that would curl your hair. Being inclusive may be the least of it. Taking the Bible seriously may be ridiculed. And to believe that Christ is the only way to salvation might be viewed as narrow and intolerant. She may hear that humans aren't really sinful at all, or if so, only when she fails to love herself enough by following her own desires and dreams.

A few years ago I got a call from a friend who was in tears over the subject matter of her teen daughter's Episcopal church youth group. The kids were viewing the film, *The Last Temptation of Christ*, produced by Martin Scorcese. It depicts Christ as doubtful about his divinity, desiring God to forgive him for his sins and leave him alone, and obsessed with Mary Magdalene (portrayed as a prostitute). Judas Iscariot is the noble hero in this film. It's just one more example of the many activities of youth groups over the years that, sadly, present a blasphemous message to vulnerable teens, steering them directly away from a close relationship with the authentic Christ.

One of the major speakers at a controversial "Re-Imagining God" feminist conference in Minneapolis in 1993, ordained Lutheran feminist Chung Hyun Kyung, ridiculed the Genesis account of the fall by taking a bite out of an apple at the podium. Apples were then passed out to the several thousand others at the conference.[9] This rebellious attitude is unfortunately not an isolated incident, but increasingly common to many of today's "Christian" clergy who are in charge of teen groups and camps for our youth.

This highly controversial conference was attended by ministers and representatives from most mainline denominations, including the Presbyterian Church USA, the United Methodist Church, the Evangelical Lutheran Church in America, the United Church of Christ, the Roman Catholic Church, the Episcopal Church, and others. Conference participants celebrated a mock communion of milk and honey offered to the goddess "Sophia," which is the Greek word for wisdom, said to be biblical because wisdom is an attribute of God in the book of Proverbs. Speakers also scoffed at doctrines such as the incarnation and atonement, and praised lesbianism.[10] Several additional "Re-Imagining" conferences were held in subsequent years.

Such views are becoming mainstream. One of the participants, Rev. Peg Chemberlin, is executive director of the Minnesota Council of Churches, which boasts membership of twenty denominations representing 23 percent of Minnesota's population.[11] Yet Rev. Peg attended that first "Re-Imagining" conference, and her positive reflections were published in an essay about the event.[12]

But honoring a goddess won't shock most of our children now. Kids are being drilled at church camps and at youth group meetings, reinforcing what they are told at school, that they are to honor the Earth as a divine or semidivine entity. One Sunday in April is set aside in many mainline congregations to celebrate Earth Day. Concepts of "eco-justice," "sustainable" living, and animal rights abound in church youth group curricula, many of which agree with the principles of the United Nations' Earth Charter:

> 12. Uphold the right of all, without discrimination, to a natural and social environment supportive of human dignity, bodily health, and spiritual well-being, with special attention to the rights of indigenous peoples and minorities. . . . b. Affirm the right of indigenous peoples to their spirituality, knowledge, lands, and resources, and to their related practice of sustainable livelihoods.[13]

This might sound innocuous until one understands that our children are taught, through this affirmation of global spiritual "rights," that they are intolerant if they believe that one way (i.e., Christianity) is better than others. The Earth Charter is widely accepted, though, and incorporated into many youth educational programs.

Everything is holy and creation itself is to be worshipped rather than worshipping the Creator as we are told in the first commandment and Romans chapter 1. The Presbyterian Church USA Web site provides its denomination's bottom line on what we are to worship:

"We are called to worship God with all our being and actions, and to treat creation as sacred."[14]

But the Bible tells us that only God is sacred—not His creation. This is a critical distinction between Christianity and earth-based pagan beliefs, and if our denominational leaders don't have it right, how can they instruct children and protect them from a pop culture enamored with a sensational, yet false, worship?

To refer to God in the masculine has also become sexist and evil. Each of us is made in the image of God, but this is often twisted to say that God can be expressed as male or female, and that each human is "god," with personal divinity just waiting to be discovered. Most parents may not realize that this is the core element of paganism.

Worship of an idea of a "goddess" is a belief among many pagans, but how it is understood is important for parents to discern. Donna Steichen, in her book *Ungodly Rage: The Hidden Face of Catholic Feminism*, explains that most followers of witchcraft "prefer a feminine deity, revealed only in human experience; they encounter her in their own impulses and worship her by obeying them."[15] This is why paganism appeals to today's spoiled American youth. It finds a spiritual rationale for doing just about anything one wishes. *What a great religion*, the uninformed adolescent will think.

And if a child escapes indoctrination at church or high school, once he reaches college, he will encounter this philosophy everywhere he turns, particularly in religion studies, which have been largely taken over by aficionados of gnostic neo-paganism and non-Christian religions. Harvard Divinity School, once dedicated to producing ministers to spread the gospel of Jesus Christ, now proudly hosts conferences on feminist theology, including goddess worshippers and "transgendered" speakers.[16] The school boasts on its Web site about its new labyrinth.[17] The labyrinth is a tool of medieval mystics, a circuitous maze pattern traced out on a walkway or stone floor. The practice involves walking the maze slowly while repeating phrases, called "prayer," but it's more like the mantra of Eastern religions. The meditation often produces a trance-like altered state of consciousness, which becomes a pathway for occult influence and is markedly different from Christian prayer.

My daughter, a 2003 graduate of a small liberal arts college, told me about an experience in one of her religion classes when her professor turned out the lights and instructed students to lie on the floor with the goal of "emptying their minds." Another course about world religions required the text *Living in the Lap of the Goddess* by Cynthia Eller, which tracks the growth of feminist spirituality and is very favorable toward witchcraft. Only a few cursory lectures about Christianity and Judaism were included in this course, which focused primarily on non-Western religions. One assignment called for pairs of students to develop a "ritual" to the goddess of their choice and lead the class in it. In other words, these students were given college credit for spell casting.

Pagan Rites vs. Christian Rights

Christians who have not been faithful to biblical principles nor active in witnessing to their secular neighbors have left a vacuum for spiritual darkness to fill. An openly hostile climate toward traditional Christianity now prevails in America, corrupting the church from within, as well as drastically limiting its influence on the culture.

The American Left has been anxious to silence orthodox Christian voices, with carefully crafted nonsense that appeals to youth lacking spiritual discernment and their uncritical parents. In coming years the ACLU, People for the American Way, and emerging pagan legal groups such as the Witches' Anti-Defamation League will achieve increasing successes as they defend the expression of alternate spirituality in American culture while restricting religious freedom for Christians. Under such a culture, Christians will become increasingly marginalized.

Recently, the Veterans Administration agreed to allow pentacles symbolizing witchcraft to be placed on the headstones of veterans who were Wiccans. This action followed a lawsuit alleging violation of religious freedom by the relatives of deceased veterans.[18]

Positive visibility of pagans in high places is helping to create a glamorized image. When I disputed the worth of the Harry Potter books in an interview on MSNBC several years ago, my witch opponent defending her craft was not a crone but was attractive and smiling as she smoothly explained that the "craft" emphasizes love, peace, and goodness.

Regular listeners of National Public Radio will be familiar with Margot Adler, a reporter on social issues and current events, who's also a producer in their New York bureau. A lesser-known fact about Adler is that she's well known in witchcraft circles as the author of *Drawing Down the Moon: Witches, Druids, Goddess-Worshippers, and Other Pagans in America Today*—a best-selling book about modern witchcraft.

But Adler is not unique; more and more professionals and others in responsible positions are "coming out" as pagans or in support of their cause. A brief controversy erupted in 2007 when a Christian policy group revealed that the chair of the Democratic Party in Kennebec County, Maine, was openly pagan. But the Christian group, not the goddess-worshipper, became the bad guy, as even the female president of Chicago Theological Seminary jumped to the pagan's defense.[19]

To the mainstream media, being a witch has little shock value anymore. Even many Christian parents show little regard or concern for the practice. Open practitioners of witchcraft and uncensored discussion have created a flood of new and casual initiates. The barriers are down because Christians have failed to preserve their influence in the culture and are, themselves, suppressing any alarm bells that may be going off.

There's an element of testing here about where our priorities and loyalties lie. When you hear the words "pagan" or "witchcraft" in connection with your kids, what does your Christian gut instinct tell you? As a concerned parent you give your kids a Bible and have them learn the first commandment that they are to worship no entity but God. Then you have them read that "witchcraft is rebellion" (1 Sam.15:23) and that practices such as sorcery and divination (trying to foresee the future) are abominations to God (Deut. 18).

Then what? With those same parental hands, you turn around and buy for them books packed with sorcery, fortune-telling, and "magick." Now multiply these books with their Christless plots and flirtation with the occult, time and again, as your avid-reading child traverses the preteen and teen years. Does anyone doubt this will have an impact on this child's spirituality? *These practices can't be all that offensive to God,* a child may think, *if my parents are okay with it.*

Why aren't more parents willing to say no? One reason is that Christians—those who should know better—are much more influenced than they should be by political correctness and the desire to avoid the "fundamentalist" label. They don't want to be one of those despised members of the religious right going out on the much-feared "witch hunt."

The task before us is to get our priorities straight and courageously show our kids the value of truth and the Christian worldview. We must teach them how to be discerning about spiritual evil and to question the growing cacophony of voices that would lead them away from Christ.

If some form of paganism becomes the preferred spiritual practice, there will be no room for an "exclusive" belief in one Savior. Worshipping Christ openly in a church might become a vague memory of an idyllic past.

There's only so far one can retreat from Satan. As the sworn enemy of Christ, Satan's main objective is to separate humans from the love of Christ through any means possible. He has never left the Lord's followers alone, but strikes when defenses are down. To assure the Christian faith of your children and grandchildren, and their ability to practice it openly, as parents, you must teach them to recognize the devices of the enemy. Some of these challenges can become fodder for deeper faith and opportunities to share the hope of Christ.

CHAPTER 2

Do What You Will: The Core Tenets of the New Spirituality

"*I was born for this,* she thought. *I can do anything.* 'Dark Mother, Queen of the Ghostways, I call thee!' cried Bethany. 'Great Mother, She who protects Her hidden children, come now into this circle and aid us in this rite!' The others replied, 'So mote it be'" (*Witches' Night Out,* 22).

* * *

"*They can't be real, Witches don't exist, there are not such things,* I thought. Only later, when I was in ninth grade, did I learn how wrong I really was" (*Spellcasting for Teens,* xvii).

If your teen daughter is looking for a quick read, she may stroll down to Borders and bring home a popular book from the *Daughter of the Moon* series by Lynne Ewing. Yes, the characters struggle with typical teen angst over clothes, school, friendships, parents, and boys. They also struggle with using their "powers" appropriately.

You see, these girls are goddesses. Yes, that's right. Serena reads your mind; Tianna moves objects through telekinesis; Vanessa becomes invisible; Jimena gets premonitions; and Catty does time travel. When they wonder about the future, they may consult tarot cards or a psychic, or gain comfort from a cherished magical amulet. But they always have to be alert for the invisible shape-shifting Followers who may attack out of nowhere. This is, of course, when they are not talking with boyfriends about whether they are ready to have sex yet or getting their latest adorable nose ring or tasteful tattoo.[1]

> *"For such are false apostles, deceitful workers, transforming themselves into apostles of Christ. And no wonder! For Satan himself transforms himself into an angel of light"* (2 Cor. 11:13–14).

These books are not *The Wizard of Oz*, where houses fly, scarecrows talk, and cities are made of emeralds—until a sweet, innocent young girl wakes up from her dream. Ewing's characters operate in a pretty much everyday world that American youth can recognize. Girls anguish over makeup, clothes, and bad hair days. The only difference is that "magick" is used by these young heroines to deal with mostly ordinary life issues.

Our children can now be tutored in pagan practices as they become part of a growing acceptance in a fearless culture. It's no wonder most American kids today don't recoil in horror when a friend says he or she is a witch. Clueless about Christian doctrine and with more and more self-proclaimed pagans in almost every corner of their world, few kids feel any trepidation about such beliefs.

Yet Scripture could not be more stern in its condemnation of pagan practices:

> *"I am the lord your God, who brought you out of the land of Egypt, out of the house of bondage. You shall have no other gods before me. You shall not make for yourself a carved image—any likeness of anything that is in heaven above, or that is in the earth beneath, or that is in the water under the earth; you shall not bow down to them nor serve them"* (Exod. 20:2–4).

* * *

"There shall not be found among you anyone who makes his son or daughter pass through the fire, or one who practices witchcraft, or a soothsayer, or one who interprets omens, or a sorcerer, or one who conjures spells, or a medium, or a spiritist, or one who calls up the dead. For all who do these things are an abomination to the Lord" (Deut. 18:10–12).

The Invisible Battle

In our material, Western world, many people have trouble with the idea of a *real* spiritual realm. Yet most other cultures in the world accept this as fact, and Scripture clearly describes this reality. The Holy Spirit, after all, is the Spirit of our Christian deity. If one believes He exists, why not heed the rest of Scripture as it paints a picture for us of the whole universe of supernatural beings?

Accepting this model of the unseen world has huge implications for mystics, pagans, and Wiccans, and what they believe, because it points toward an enormous *lie*. No one wants to face the crumbling edifice of a false faith.

Yet there is a deliberate and unrelenting battle to deceive people. Scripture says that Satan and his army of fallen (demonic) spirits are real. Satan is a "roaring lion, seeking whom he may devour" (1 Pet. 5:8). Jesus said he is also a murderer and a liar (John 8:44). But in everyday experience, how does this work?

The best way to describe it is in terms of a battle of ideas and feelings. Our primary struggle does not consist of flesh and blood, but it is against "spiritual hosts of wickedness in the heavenly places" (Eph. 6:12).

Satan's goals are to separate people forever from God. How does this happen? At some level of thoughts and spiritual input, this enemy uses a person's own tendency to sin and amplifies it. Satan and his army of fallen angels do have influence on an individual's thought life, particularly upon unbelievers or those who are not walking closely with God.

So, in a battle, a clever foe will use whatever works. Satan's tactics fall into several categories:

- Deception
- Dissension
- Distraction
- Destruction

Deception may appear in many forms. The original sin in the Garden of Eden was the pride of not trusting God, of doubting His wonderful provision, and of letting curiosity to be like Him overrule His instruction. Satan in the form of the serpent whispered these ideas to Eve, and Adam did not disagree. And so it began.

Sin is, therefore, portrayed as enticing, ego-building, consequence-free—and the key to happiness. Frequently, the sin involves a person becoming his or her own boss, not God. False faiths will be appealing mainly because the control seems to be in the hands of the individual through worldly actions, rituals, and good deeds.

The ultimate lie is discounting, distrusting, distorting, or even hating God Almighty and Jesus Christ. This movement away from God with its *dissension* among people is fertile ground for the enemy to work.

If all else fails, Satan will use the *distraction* of worldly cares and self-focused concerns to keep people from carefully evaluating what they believe and why. And ultimately, Satan will level a final assault of *destruction* of the person in physical and/or spiritual terms.

What Is a Pagan?

In this context, current neo-pagan trends need to be seen for what they are. They are not "progressive" new spiritual insights, but are as old as humanity. It should not be a surprise that Satan is especially interested in misleading young people.

In defining paganism and current witchcraft, considerable disagreement exists among today's practitioners about what a "pagan" or "witch" is. Among the e-mails I receive, many argue vehemently that "Wicca" is this or it's not that.

"You don't understand our beliefs at all!" is a frequent refrain.

What is really meant is that I don't see it from their viewpoint, and that's, of course, true. From a pagan worldview, a person is free to construct a faith shaped however they wish, and then they operate as if it's real. But from the Christian viewpoint, there is a big gap between pagan beliefs and truth itself.

Those involved in sorcery usually don't grasp what it is they are doing and why it's a problem. A few pagans do understand and have made their choice anyway for their own purposes. Yet deliberate rebellion versus default rebellion through ignorance may serve to describe the state of one's heart, but in biblical terms, each person is still responsible. Rebellion is still rebellion.

Paganism and witchcraft didn't make much sense until I became a Christian. Then the patterns, practices, and ultimate error of paganism came into sharp focus through its contrast with Christian principles. Like a knockoff designer dress hung next to a genuine one, the distinctions become obvious and glaring.

Because of this, I define paganism as the practice of attempting to harness the power of the supernatural for one's own purposes, and the power being sought is deliberately, sometimes defiantly Christless, with no room for "inclusion" of our Almighty God.

What's the Attraction?

Pagans historically have had trouble being taken seriously because many people dismiss their beliefs as goofy. They're either flakes or fakes, has been the prevailing view. But that's quickly changing. Our children don't always have that prejudice. In fact, many young people think it's chic or trendy to try on a Wiccan or pagan identity. "Spirituality" is in, for good or ill.

Yet attempt to debate with most young pagans, to talk with them about the evidence for truth, and you'll get a standard response: "Well, you have no right to criticize my beliefs. If your faith works for you, fine; but my faith works for me, so leave it alone." It's as if some-one had commented on a new hairstyle.

The "pagan worldview" is appealing for reasons other than its truthfulness. This postmodern generation does not like hard facts or believe they matter. Being a pagan appears to allow a person to be in charge and change the rule book at will. It offers the tantalizing promise of mysticism, and it guarantees sexual self-determination. You don't have to worry about evangelizing, so you can totally focus on what's in it for yourself. For feminists, it claims to be egalitarian. And it revels in sensual experience, in glorifying the erotic, the beautiful in nature and in yourself. On the face of it, there seems to be no reason to resist. It sounds too good to be true.

And, of course, it is. Ultimate lies and traps are buried here—the primary one being the illusion that *you* are in charge. If the God of the Bible exists, if Christ is, indeed, Savior, then goddess worshippers and sorcerers are in real trouble.

The practices that accompany pagan beliefs vary widely. At the most casual level, some are simply interested in the ritual, the community, and the lifestyle of liberation. The more involved practitioner will be raising power; casting spells; practicing divination through astrology or tarot cards; meditating; and using other occult techniques in hopes of gaining supernatural knowledge and power.

Many parents and adults believe correctly that it is possible for a teen to be involved in these activities but not make contact with a "spirit" at all. Since it has a growing favorable reputation, particularly in more liberal circles, there are many "bubblegum" witches out there—young teens who are trying on paganism as today's current costuming. However, this does not mean it's harmless. The teen who just downloads a couple of spells from a Web site, tosses together a few herbs, and lights a candle in his or her room still faces spiritual accountability, starting with not worshipping God Almighty.

It is clear that some seekers do make spiritual contact, and this is the ever-present danger, as is the rebellious attitude toward God that prompts this exploration in the first place.

The Source of Pagan Power

There are several primary ideas among pagans about where they think power originates. The individual pagan, with others in a coven, grove, or circle, or as a sole practitioner, can call upon this power and then direct it to a specific use. The power as they envision it may emanate from one or more presumed deities (goddesses and/or gods), or a more generalized all-powerful deity. Again, in the pagan's mind, none of these deities will resemble the Christian Almighty God, nor is there any place among these deities for a Savior like Christ.[2] Of course, a few pagans will call on "God" or "Jesus," but it soon becomes clear that they have a completely different "Jesus" in mind than the King of Kings.

Some pagans or witches may also ascribe to the Hindu concept of a universal force connecting a polytheistic realm, with higher and higher degrees of possible spiritual achievement. It's very common for pagans to believe in reincarnation. The nonspecific Great God may also resemble the primary deity of many Native Americans. There is a whole American arm of witchcraft that follows the image of the female shaman, or "medicine woman," as popularized by Lynn Andrews, author of *Medicine Woman* and *Teachings Around the Sacred Wheel* (HarperSanFrancisco, 1983 and 1989), among others.

Another common view is that the power comes *from within oneself*, and is really part of an untapped energy source—a "higher order thinking," or the unused portions of one's brain. The prolific witch writer Starhawk (a.k.a. Miriam Simos) says this energy resembles what the Chinese call "chi." It "flows in certain patterns throughout the human body, and can be raised, stored, shaped, and sent."[3] This recalls elements of Jungian psychology with its "collective unconscious" and archetypal myths.[4] The irony is that believing one is a god was the original sin of Adam and Eve. Such profound implications still fail to move many pagans, who brazenly plunge ahead into the current iteration of ancient heresy.

A combination of these two viewpoints (external vs. internal source) is common among witches, the internal power usually linked with a female deity ("the goddess in you"). Or an unnamed force may reside in all things, stored in animals, plants, rocks, trees, and even one's computer or clothing. The arrangement of home furnishings in a specific way to utilize this all-pervasive energy is even the foundation of a neo-pagan interior decorating method called feng shui, which incorporates earth-based pagan beliefs.[5]

And usually witches maintain that power can be "good" or "evil," the idea of white witchcraft vs. black magic. Modern witchcraft has a saying, probably developed by Gerald Gardner in the 1950s[6] even though it sounds medieval: *"An ye harm none, do what you will."* As you will see, the authority on what constitutes "harm" is the individual sorcerer, whose decisions can accommodate various needs and situations.

Peter Jones, PhD, has written several profoundly insightful books about the American and global descent into paganism. He believes the current interest in witchcraft is the latest manifestation of alternate spirituality, fueled by popular feminist political goals. In his book *Gospel Truth/Pagan Lies,* he summarizes the five principles of gnostic/pagan belief:

- All is one and one is all—the universe is God.
- Humanity is one, all connected.
- All religions are one.
- One real problem—good vs. evil, male vs. female, should be resolved by unification, or blurring of absolutes.
- One solution: we save ourselves, through meditation or recognition of our own divinity.[7]

The flexibility of this belief system resonates with today's youth, especially in America. Though structurally unsound, it allows the appearance of religious faith while retaining the option to binge on the blessings of affluence, peace, and prosperity. Since the biblical foundation of American life and our nation's fruitfulness are intertwined, as individuals feed on rotten spiritual nourishment, their well-being may deteriorate along with that of the nation.

The central issue is reality. The Christian faith is based on historical events and spiritual truth revealed from God, and teaches principles that are in direct opposition to the neo-pagan view. This precludes blending the two faiths. Christians would say that, sadly, the "power" felt by the pagan is the person's own sinfulness in contact with the demonic spiritual realm. These demonic spirits can disguise themselves as necessary to gain entry into an individual's life (as in 2 Cor. 11:14). They can be your dead Uncle Harry, Alexander the Great, one's own personal spirit guide, a beloved saint, or even a false "Jesus."

Very few pagans acknowledge anything like this and will emphatically state that they do not worship Satan. Christians would maintain that, in essence, it is Satan's army of demonic spirits that ritualists contact, even if they do not realize it.

Margot Adler, a well-known witchcraft author, seems most attracted to the notion that witchcraft power arises from a person's own mind. She accepted the idea of witchcraft after idealizing Greek goddesses as a child and then as an adult listening to a tape in which they were honored as the "Great Mother": "A feeling of power and emotion came over me . . . The contents of the tape had simply given me permission to accept a part of my own psyche that I had denied for years."[8] Her own desires were the guide, not objective facts and evidence. In fact, a rejection of logic in favor of one's own personal experiences and needs is a central theme in paganism. Truth is just another power play, women's studies professors tell their female students, based on the patriarchy that is the *real* sin.[9]

The Myth of Matriarchy

Paganism, along with one of its more mainstream labels, "feminist spirituality," is exploding in popularity because its history fits with the current social goals of equality and civil rights—or so it seems.

It is claimed that ancient, peace-loving, sexually liberated matriarchal cultures once worshipped a "Mother Goddess," along with her consort, a horned god. They assert that about 35,000 years ago these groups were usurped by militant hordes that followed male gods (like Yahweh, then Christ). Archaeology has purportedly found evidence of these paleo-European civilizations in squat female figurines, drawings of spirals, suns, and moons attuned to the seasonal cycle of growth and harvest, as well as human fertility. Rituals were performed (it is believed) that resemble current witchcraft "spells." Supposedly this whole belief system was then forced underground after a period of persecution during the Middle Ages and the burning of perhaps as many as nine million people, mostly women, during the Inquisition conducted by the Holy Roman church.[10]

Yet there's little evidence such matriarchies existed. Many ancient cultures did worship goddesses, not exclusively, but rather alongside male gods. Priestesses sometimes served as temple prostitutes who performed sexual rites along with religious rituals, a fact frequently mentioned in the Old Testament in descriptions of pagan nations surrounding Israel and, later, of unfaithful Israel itself. Male prostitutes are also mentioned (Deut. 23:17, 18; 2 Kings 23:7). There's also not much evidence that a goddess was preeminent.

Nor is there evidence these cultures were peaceful, and certainly little evidence for societies ruled by women. And while suspected witches were imprisoned and executed during the Middle Ages, there is little to support a figure as extreme as nine million. More careful researchers put the figure at around 40,000 over many centuries. Many of these were men.[11]

Several scholars have taken serious issue with theories of a dominant pre-Christian matriarchy. Philip G. Davis in his book, *Goddess Unmasked: The Rise of Neopagan Feminist Spirituality*, carefully debunks, culture by culture, the archaeological support for these claims. He also traces the rise in the twentieth-century interest in goddess worship and witchcraft not to an age-old tradition resurfacing, but to twentieth-century writings of proponents such as Elizabeth Gould Davis, Gerald Gardner, Merlin Stone, Riane Eisler, Michael Dames, Naomi Goldenberg, Marija Gimbutas, and others. More likely, current "witchcraft" is an amorphous brew of folk customs, occult spirituality, and pop New Age trends. For other details which won't be repeated here, I would suggest reviewing this portion of Davis's book.[12]

In assessing the claims, Davis notes there is not "a single translated text from any of the most important goddess cultures to tell us what these ancient people actually believed."[13] After reviewing the excavations of sites in Malta, Catal Huyuk (Turkey), the Balkans, ancient Britain, the Indus Valley, and Crete,[14] Davis came to the following conclusion:

> The findings of our investigation . . . indicate that none of the societies most often cited as authentic ancient Goddess cultures actually conforms to our expectations. Not a single one provides clear evidence of a single, supreme female deity; not a single one exhibits the signs of matriarchal rule. . . . In each of these cases, the story of the Goddess is a fabrication in defiance of the facts.[15]

In contrast to the popular matriarchy myth, when one reviews the elements of ancient pagan cultures as revealed by credible archaeology, they are consistent with descriptions found in the Old and New Testaments. From the traditional Christian and Jewish viewpoint, ancient paganism much more likely arose originally from rebellion against Almighty God and His laws. And it's happening again where one might least expect—in wealthy, God-blessed twenty-first-century America.

The Use of Power through "Magick"

Not all pagans experience connection with supernatural forces. Some people simply call themselves pagans, witches, or "Wiccans" because of sympathy with feminism, ecology, or other lifestyle or political views.

But others do attempt to contact the spiritual realm, and the more persistent succeed. Adults who dismiss paganism as a stylistic trend or rebellious adolescent stage need a wake-up call, because *something* supernatural is frequently happening, and it's happening with more and more people in America.

Margot Adler gives an account in her book, *Drawing Down the Moon,* of how a group of dabblers in occult practices tried the same ritual three times. The third time, a nonintellectual force took hold and "it worked!"[16] Similarly, former witch Kathleen Ward Atchason provides stern warnings about dabbling with sorcery. She believes many women experiment with the practice and are naïve about its power. Another ex-witch, Paula Keene, tries to warn people about the danger. "Magic is real and it works," she says.[17]

The actual practice of sorcery is what today's neo-pagans call "magick" or "ritual," and these are really terms for spells. This is not like Christian prayer for many reasons. One is that various props, such as herbs, candles, wands, and incense are utilized. The activity is performed in a sequence of steps. Such spells vary greatly, and pagans can invent their own spells.

Pagans can work alone or in a group, which is called a coven, grove, or a circle, so named because of the form a ritual often takes— gathering in a circle. Spells can include chanting, dancing, drumming, drugs, or even, in some cases, sexual activity. The intensity of the group actions build, which practitioners call "raising energy." It gathers to a peak, called a "cone of power," often accompanied by more serious practitioners with an altered state of consciousness among the head priestess, priest, and others in the group. This is the point it is believed where the "power" can be focused with the aid of a named deity and then "sent" toward an intended recipient or goal. Hence the term, "casting" a spell.

The objective is to make a change—get a desired job, lover, grade on a test, date for the prom, money in one's bank account, and so on. The idea of prayer to Almighty God and trusting Him with whatever outcome He decides is not at all compatible with the mind-set of the pagan practitioner. The pagan *wants*, therefore has to make it happen on his or her timetable. It gets down to an issue of control directed by the self, through the ritual actions and intentions.

Specific spells are available in growing numbers of books and on many Web sites. A spell usually incorporates props. The pagan believes certain activities must be done in a specific order with candles, incense, herbs, and so on in order to make the spell "work." In the mind-set of the practitioner, she has bought into a system of "magical thinking," which is the antithesis of Christian belief.

The magical mind believes, like superstitious pagans of primitive cultures, that there is a "correspondence" between what takes place in the material world and what takes place on the supernatural plane. So, to manipulate that other world, one has to perform little plays down here on earth. Dancing to bring rain, meditating on poppets, or sticking pins in voodoo dolls are examples of this acting out. Pagan thinking also maintains that sheer intensity of force, focused on the desired goal, will also produce a desired outcome.[18]

This mind-set trusts in symbols and patterns to a superstitious degree. So the labyrinth now being used for prayer and meditative walking even in many nominally Christian churches, is believed to carry power simply in its structure. It's a "sacred pattern," according to Lauren Artress, the female minister who brought a labyrinth to Grace Cathedral in San Francisco: "To walk a sacred path is to discover our inner sacred space: that core of feeling that is waiting to have life breathed back into it through symbols, archetypal forms like the labyrinth, rituals, stories and myth."[19]

Artress believes that God is not a separate being from humanity, that He is not transcendent, but God is within each person, and certain patterns release our discovery of that self-divinity. Despite the fact that she functions in a Christian church, Artress is expressing purely pagan, non-Christian beliefs.

Words or numbers can carry a lot of power and significance, the pagan believes. So the number three that repeats itself during one day and again in a person's dream, can be interpreted as a message from the divine. Language that is "negative" or that doesn't express what the pagan likes is not to be mentioned, because to say something gives it power. I've had pagans write to me and say that they don't acknowledge Satan, because to do so would give him power.

This is classic superstitious thinking that can become bondage for the person who is constantly looking for, and then responding to, certain symbols, words, and messages. By contrast, Christianity frees the individual from such confusion.

Another act of "correspondence" by a ritual group can involve sexual rites. The goal is a consummation here on earth of a desired objective in the spirit realm. It can serve as an old-fashioned fertility rite. It can also be a means of initiation, or a method for achieving an altered state of consciousness. Teen witch writer Gwinevere Rain mentions the possibility of doing rituals "sky-clad"—the pagan term for nudity.[20] Modern witchcraft "founding father" Gerald Gardner was quite open about his affinity for nudity[21] and many witchcraft writers have been quite open about the acceptability of "sex magic" as a part of coven gatherings. Among these are Margot Adler,[22] Miriam Simos (Starhawk),[23] Susan Bowes,[24] Doreen Valiente, Scott Cunningham,[25] and Patricia Monaghan.[26]

Rituals are the core purpose of earth-based paganism, the focus of "worship," if you will. There are important dates, called "Sabbats," that pagans and witches celebrate that correspond to ancient pagan holidays. Samhain (pronounced *sow-in* or *sow-een*), the pagan "new year" and its most significant day, falls on October 31, Halloween. Imbolc, or Candlemas, is February 2, a festival of light. The ancient fertility festival of Beltane falls on May 1, which corresponds to May Day. Lammas or Lughnasa is August 1 and is the celebration of the first of the harvest. There are four lesser sabbats—the two solstices (winter, December 21, and summer, June 21) and the two equinoxes (spring, March 21, and autumn, September 21).[27]

Other than spells, paganism employs an array of other occult activities. Fortune-telling (divination) through astrology, tarot cards, crystals, or other means is common. Charms or amulets are often retained for good fortune. Some pagans seek contact with what they believe are "familiars," or animals and the spirits believed to inhabit them. The goal is to harness this spirit and target it to a specific objective.

Are pagans "Satanists"? Do they practice child sacrifice? There are some sensational accounts along these lines. That is not the purpose here. Even though the powers involved ultimately have a connection to the spiritual evil of Satan, so do many other God-avoiding distractions of the secular world. The vast majority of people practicing paganism will not get to these extreme levels, and any attempts to have a meaningful discussion with these neo-pagans will be derailed by wild accusations. This in no way minimizes the danger of occult practices and the profoundly negative consequences in the lives of practitioners and those close to them.

Disinformation and Delusion

In order to be seduced into paganism, the young mind must be impressionable enough to adopt its worldview. The concepts that shape this worldview can be summarized as follows:

- Focus on *self*, will, and pride
- Focus on immediate gratification
- Preference for sensual pleasure over virtue and idealism
- Fascination with the mysterious and dangerous
- A bias *against* Christianity

The youth who has been propped up with inflated self-esteem, indulged from birth, provided shortcuts to avoid learning patience and diligence, and tantalized with sensational entertainment will naturally gravitate toward paganism. What seals the bargain is to prevent this child from seriously evaluating the message of Christianity, which could bring truth, light, goodness, and humility to his life.

Supporters of pagan values often foment anti-Christian attitudes by conveying half-truths and misinformation about God, the Bible, and believers. Seldom do the advocates of pagan beliefs debate the core issues: point for point, Christian beliefs vs. pagan beliefs, Christ vs. Mother Earth, or gnostic secret knowledge.

Virtually every pagan publication or Web site contains a "Christian-bashing" section. No other faith gets this kind of treatment. It stands to reason, however, since Christianity is the primary obstacle facing those who practice sorcery.

Consider this core belief of many pagans, repeated in Silver Ravenwolf's book, *Teen Witch: Wicca for a New Generation*: "Our only animosity toward Christianity, or toward any other religion or philosophy of life, is to the extent that these institutions have claimed to be 'the one true right and only way' and have sought to deny freedom to others and to suppress other ways of religious practices and belief."[28]

Patricia Monaghan's *Wild Girls: The Path of the Young Goddess* introduces girls to pagan mythology from many cultures while providing a tutorial in pagan traditions. She writes, "It became clear to me that girls from our culture who have a monotheistic view of God who is always described as 'He' must struggle much harder to find the 'God within' than their male counterparts, who can identify with 'Him.'"[29] She misrepresents the Christian faith, which never teaches that God is automatically "within" a person, but a separate being Who will indwell believing humans yet always remain a distinct, almighty entity. God (the Holy Spirit) indwells only those who accept Christ as Savior.

She adds to the confusion by asserting that the purpose of lighting candles on Christmas Eve is "to celebrate and sustain the inner light of holiness within each of us that corresponds to the Christ child." It's as "magical a ritual as any Wiccan ceremony."[30] Most American children don't have the depth of Christian education to immediately discern the error in such breezy comparisons. Too many will accept witchcraft as compatible with Christianity.

Margot Adler is much more openly hostile. "The fundamentalist impulse . . . is, along with nuclear war, the most dangerous peril facing the human race."[31]

Our children are hearing the most virulent antagonism against Christianity, however, by goddess-worshippers, radical feminists, and pagans operating *within* Christian denominations. Discarding the Bible's authority and undermining faithfulness to its tenets is job number one for these mutineers.

Lauren Artress, ordained minister at Grace Cathedral in San Francisco and advocate of the tolerance and peace that can be found through the labyrinth, has zero tolerance for biblical faithfulness:

> As fear for our individual as well as collective future increases, the flight into a literal interpretation of the Bible is experiencing a dramatic revival. This fear breeds small-mindedness and mean-spiritedness. . . . The punishment of people who do not follow the rules is becoming more predominant. . . . The shadow of the human spirit that led to Hitler and World War II stalks us once again.[32]

The bitter, some would say blasphemous, words of revolutionary feminists pepper many essays, speeches, and books. Elizabeth A. Johnson writes in *She Who Is*:

> In the Christian community . . . for most of its history women have been subordinated in theological theory and ecclesial practice at every turn. . . . They are called to honor a male savior sent by a male god whose legitimate representatives can only be male. . . . This process is strongly aided and abetted by male-centered language and symbol systems.[33]

The first step toward an answer to this "problem" for Johnson and other radicals in Christian churches is to change the language. Therefore, God becomes a "She," or a goddess, or we can even name ourselves as "gods." Such arbitrary ideas have standing with these women superior to the inspired Word of God.

What does set the parameters of faith for these neo-pagans is their own *experience*. Rita Gross, religious studies professor and feminist, sums it up: "Since women have been largely excluded from androcentric theology and religious leadership, *women's experiences* need to be discovered, recovered, and taken seriously. When that is done, a *new naming of reality* begins to occur [italics in the original]."[34]

Defecting in Place is a book about women who have remained within Christian churches while also practicing goddess-worship and/or pagan ritual. "Language is so powerful that to refer to my Creator as Mother, Grandmother of all, Goddess, has changed how I will live forever," an American Baptist clergywoman is quoted as saying. An Episcopalian woman says, "Though we use feminine terms for God in our home, the children hear the traditional God the Father much too often."[35]

This book, if accurate, indicates that the nation's Christian churches are replete with female members already involved in practicing pagan rituals in church-sponsored women's groups. Youth groups in such churches are no doubt exposed to this paganized "Christianity" as well.

Changing the faith by language and experience need not follow any particularly logical path, either. Donna Steichen calls this "religion as psychology" and quotes Naomi Goldenberg, a religious feminist, as bluntly admitting this: "A remembered fact and an invented fantasy have identical psychological value. . . . Modern witches are using religion and ritual as psychological tools."[36]

So along with a primitive return to throwing salt over one's shoulder and not stepping on cracks for fear of breaking Mother's back, our children are being convinced that truth is unknowable or irrelevant. And since, again, words are believed to have intrinsic power, only those ideas a person likes should be expressed—or allowed to be expressed—aloud.

Witch Laurie Cabot writes, "Wording your spell correctly is important. Words are powerful instruments in and of themselves."[37] *Teen Witch* author Silver Ravenwolf says, "We believe that to give evil a name is to give evil power."[38] Patricia Monaghan tells girls who become practitioners of magic to be careful about the power of words. "Like any ritual, the repetition of words affects us . . . words bear messages to our deep mind, from which change is born."[39]

One related belief is the notion of shaping and creating God by *our* actions. This idea was named process theology and developed by mathematician and philosopher Alfred North Whitehead. It has been enthusiastically incorporated into feminism and mainline Protestantism over the last few decades. Essentially, it maintains that God is changed by the actions of all creation because we are part of God. He is not a separate being, nor is He therefore omnipotent. "God" is evolving, as apparently we humans are also. Our imagination, words, and activities are forming "God."[40] As "co-creators," we are conveniently allowed to justify any desire or behavior as being part of "God." The modern pagan worldview frequently relies on this premise.

In fact, the ritual of witchcraft has change as its intention. The changes are directed at the world—including the goal of the spell itself—but also within each participant and in the goddess herself, embodying the forces of the universe. In this way, feminist radicals have decided to incite revolution at a spiritual level.

Rita Gross says, ". . . it is important to remember that ritual is more important to the feminist spirituality movement than any particular belief . . . we do not *believe* in the Goddess; we connect with Her."[41] So the youth who reveals an interest in paganism may quickly move to the *practice* of sorcery as well.

A New Definition of Sin

Reality becomes what the pagan wants it to be, as words take on new meanings. The concept of "sin," witches claim, does not exist for them. Yet pagans steadfastly maintain they have ethics and standards. As Starhawk explains it: "Witches do not see justice as administered by some external authority, based on some written code or set of rules imposed from without. Instead, justice is an inner sense that each act brings about consequences that must be faced responsibly. . . . In the Craft, all people are already seen as manifest gods."[42]

Each person—including each child or teen practitioner—is thereby "empowered" to decide on whether any given action is sinful or not. Neale Donald Walsch, New Age writer of *Conversations with God for Teens*, puts it very simply. In the book, he plays "God" as he gives wisdom like this to teens, "I do not forgive. That is the first thing you must understand about me. I will not forgive you ever, for anything you do . . . *I do not forgive anyone because there is nothing to forgive* [italics in the original]."[43] The Walsch book popularizes many of the beliefs of modern paganism. Public school students can order it through catalogs from Scholastic, Inc., distributor of Harry Potter books in the United States.

Yet this seeming benevolence is seldom extended to traditional Christians. Neo-pagans, in fact, do believe in "sin" but completely redefined, with harsh judgment meted out to patriarchy, sexism, and intolerance exhibited (they contend) by Bible-believers. And they do talk about an afterlife, but it sounds a lot like Woodstock in the clouds. Ray Buckland writes, "There is no separate 'Heaven' and 'Hell,' no 'Judgment Day,' no 'Purgatory,' no 'Eternal Damnation'! *All* go to Summerland . . . There is found rest and peace. One grows young again to eventually be reborn, through the agencies of the Goddess, into the next incarnation [italics in the original]."[44]

Does he really mean *all*—even Christians? From the adversarial stance taken by pagans and goddess-worshippers, this claim of inclusion may be suspect. At the 1998 Re-Imagining God conference in Minneapolis, Donna Hailson, an ordained minister in the American Baptist church and an expert on feminist theology was, along with several other traditional Christian women, ejected from the conference when organizers realized where their sympathies lay. In an atmosphere where goddess names were substituted for God the Father and discrimination of women was decried, there was no tolerance for the viewpoints of conservative women.[45]

Yet the girl practitioner of paganism is a "young goddess," as Patricia Monaghan calls her. She is "always free to move and explore, to follow her own heart . . . even in her heroism, she is motivated by her own drives and desires."[46] What if those "drives and desires" include resentment, rage, even a desire to harm someone else? Monaghan cautions but doesn't forbid. "About cursing: while it is sometimes tempting, when angry, to try to cast a curse or hex upon someone, be careful about giving in to such temptation. There is power in words, and it can easily loop back and hit you in the face."[47] Again it's up to the girl, who, Monaghan envisions in her introduction, may be as young as ten years old.[48]

Starhawk explains that the idea of cursing is controversial among witches. Some forbid it; others claim it's an important power to retain because it's connected to "healing," which may include stopping someone "who threatens the safety of others."[49] Some Wiccans might believe Christians are a threat. By contrast, Christ told us to love our enemies and "bless those who curse you, do good to those who hate you, and pray for those who spitefully use you and persecute you" (Matt. 5:43, 44). That would also include those who are pagans. Bringing the truth to them through education would be one important aspect of Christlike love.

Harry Potter and his friends frequently harbor desires for revenge on their enemies, and sometimes they get it. This response is seldom discouraged or punished in the Rowling books. Harry's contempt for his relatives, the Dursleys, is glorified and justified.

The Dursleys are caricatures of people with conventional values. Their worst failing is that they are "anti-magic." They're also ignorant, petty, and humorless. In *Harry Potter and the Prisoner of Azkaban*, Harry puts a hex on Aunt Marge so that her body inflates like a pig. Uncle Vernon is outraged at Harry.

"'COME BACK IN HERE!' he bellowed . . . But a reckless rage had come over Harry. 'She deserved it,' Harry said, breathing very fast. . . . You keep away from me.'"

Harry ignores his uncle and hustles away from the house to return to wizard school for another term. Aunt Marge's sin? She insulted Harry's deceased parents.[50]

If allowed, every human would have different ideas of right and wrong, as well as of justice. Since humans tend to be self-interested, these "ethics" of paganism don't lend themselves to harmonic community living for long, unless everyone in the commune is high on drugs and/or living on a trust fund. Given the stresses and strains of normal living, unchanging standards—like those of Christianity—bring stability and peace, not war.

No Leaders, No Boundaries

There is also a peace that arises from responsible leadership, heroes, and authorities who govern certain arenas of life. Yet another aspect of the pagan worldview is the ideal of perfect equality and minimal or no authority.

> I visualized Alpha and Omega, the beginning and the end, as any point on a circle. I had a keen desire to tear down crosses and put up wreaths. This God of the circle was the movement of time in the seasons and the renewal of life through birth, death, and rebirth . . . if we all have value and power, there are no leaders and followers—only sharing circles for dancing, talking, or simply belonging.

So went the reflections of one woman who attended the 1993 Re-Imagining goddess conference sponsored by Christian churches.[51]

But practically speaking, how does such a system work? Not very well, and that's yet another example of the unrealistic approach to human nature paganism forces on its adherents. Instead of allowing people to be as they are, paganism, while it sounds like freedom, really becomes a new kind of bondage. Like clothes that don't fit, the human community might struggle to make it work, but ultimately it doesn't.

Yet ideologues of paganism may not be concerned. They celebrate not just the anarchy of relativist values, but the breaking of virtually all boundaries—age, time, sex, spirit, life, even biology. Selling this to today's kids isn't very hard. Po-Ke-Mon, Yu-Gi-Oh, Shaman King, Sailor Moon, and other games and cartoons in the "anime" genre utilize a blending of living and inanimate, human and animal, in an occult tapestry, with sorcery woven in and around the action. Certain characters are warriors or shamans. Others are "familiars" captured for the use of their power by other characters. Monster characters are conjured up as needed. Certain rituals summon certain characters; others have psychic abilities. Ancient myth blends with martial arts themes. Kids are urged to collect as many of the cards representing characters as possible, in order to accumulate "power."

And if this doesn't satisfy a child's spiritual imagination, there's always the Animorphs series of books for the preteen crowd (New York: Scholastic). This series by Katherine Applegate thoroughly acquaints children with the idea of demon possession, only it's not called that. The possession is done by parasites from another planet. Five teens have the ability to defend the earth against these parasites. They can also "morph" (change) into animals, like the occult practice of shape-shifting.

When there is no sin, everything is permissible. Blasphemy no longer applies, or so the pagan mind believes. Matthew Fox, an avowed pantheist who is a defrocked Catholic priest, led "Techno-Cosmic Masses" in Oakland, California, at an abandoned ballroom. Hundreds of people, including many youths, came to one program. Reported an attendee, "Celtic music was playing as we entered the cavernous, dark ballroom. Six large video screens were placed around the room . . . In two corners . . . were small altars, pagan altars." One altar honored the Celtic goddess Brigid (not the saint of the same name) and a drawing of the Green Man, the horned god said to be the consort of the goddess.

As the service began, people sat in concentric circles in the room. Matthew Fox spoke into the microphone, "We are tired of being preached at in pews!" A small woman led the audience in pagan ritual as she "summoned" the powers of the east, west, north, and south, a procedure witches have named "calling the corners." As she did so, she thrust a dagger into the air, called an athame by witches. She spoke about Celtic spirituality, then the crowd broke into wild dancing, which continued for fifteen minutes. After being shown a film about the potato famine in Ireland, people started groaning and wailing. The music rose until it was almost deafening—then stopped. After that, a "communion" service was offered up to the goddess Brigid and to the acts of compassion that we humans do, following Christ's example. The observer left at this point, not wishing to witness such perversion of the Lord's Supper.[52]

Christian adults will have to make their own choices about how far we should "tolerate" the deceit of paganism in American life, especially in the messages of endorsement our children receive. Some adults have chosen to tell children that loyalty to the Lord means steering clear of any television show or book, cute story or not, if the tale is about youth practicing *witchcraft*.

"You will know them by their fruits" (Matt. 7:16).

CHAPTER 3

The Spiritual Consequences of Paganism

> Balthamos said quietly, "The Authority, God, the Creator, the Lord, Yahweh, El, Adonai, the King, the Father, the Almighty—these were the names he gave himself. He was never the creator. He was an angel like ourselves. . . . He told those who came after him that he created them, but it was a lie." (*The Amber Spyglass,* 31, 32)

The youth of America are being fed a steady diet of myths about God, Christian theology, and even about Jesus Christ and what He taught. They have absorbed a disturbing array of false impressions about the Christian faith:

- The highest pillar of Christianity is tolerance. "Judge not," taken out of context, is the most important idea.
- The Old Testament features a violent and oppressive God.
- Christianity teaches that everyone is basically good, self-esteem should be a high priority, and we can seek the divine within ourselves.

- Christian/Western values, derived from distorted biblical teaching, have spawned persecution, homophobia, racism, slavery, sexism, sexual repression, imperialism, and environmental destruction.
- The real Jesus loves everyone, and this love means He approves of feminism, socialism, abortion, and homosexuality. He would also have condoned many different paths to God, including paganism.

In breezy confidence, the young pagan adopts a misleading and deceptive notion about Christian faith. As a result, authentic belief is missed or dismissed; the seductive spirit of sorcery is embraced instead.

> *"Beloved, do not believe every spirit, but test the spirits, whether they are of God; because many false prophets have gone out into the world"* (1 John 4:1).

Many articulate essays and books walk through the Scripture verses refuting such false claims. However, we want to cover some basics here, knowing that the person whose ears are willing to hear can be drawn toward the nobility, justice, and ultimate freedom of the gospel message.

Our youth dive into paganism believing it will be their salvation from the presumed evils of Western, Christian culture. How cruel it will be to learn too late that this view was false and had steered them not into paradise, but off a cliff. If it's true that Jesus Christ is the Savior of the world, then the consequences of dismissing Him are enormous and eternal. Typical of postmodernists, the young pagan often diminishes the totality of who Christ was and is. Jesus opposed pagan practices, and this is a good thing for all humanity.

The Real Jesus Christ

Most false faiths carry some seeds of truth, but the test is to ask where they lead. Like any journey, it's wise to know the destination before starting out, and in faith, that's where the genuine becomes distinct from the counterfeit.

There is no other model on earth of a faith that has a God like Christianity does. The Scriptures identify Jesus Christ as God in the flesh on earth. He was fully human yet without sin. He voluntarily, humbly, and yet powerfully sacrificed Himself for His own creatures, then overcame death to demonstrate what really constitutes power, faithfulness, truth, and love.

The tangible, practical evidence to support Christianity is throughout the world—in places, traditions, archaeology, language, and the sacrifices of countless Christians. The most compelling evidence is Christ Himself—how and why He came to earth. Rather than God continuing to be separate and unseen from His creatures, Christ's birth, death, and resurrection demonstrate through historical fact and in historical time the reality of God's promises to Israel and then to the rest of humanity. As a pivotal spot on the timeline of human history, there is no comparison to the event splitting "BC" from "AD."

Christ was the Light of the World (John 8:12), the Good Shepherd (John 10:11), the Bread of Life (John 6:35). He declared to the Jews in the temple (John 8:54–58) and the woman at the well (John 4:26) that He was the Messiah. He also told Peter and some of the disciples (Mark 8:27–30), and the blind man to whom He gave sight (John 9:35–37). He did not deny Martha when she stated as much (John 11:25–27). He was, most emphatically, not simply a "good teacher" but was the Creator and Savior of all humanity.

As deity, Christ was "in the beginning . . . with God" (John 1: 1, 2). All things came to existence through the creative agency of Christ (John 1:3; Eph. 3:9; Col. 1:16). So Christ was not simply a wise man or just a prophet. He was fully able to set the parameters of sin in His eternal law, then forgive and save us from sin, since He was and is God. After granting humans total free will starting in the Garden of Eden, God also graciously provided a way for us to be reconciled to Him through the personhood of Christ.

Christ was and is the beginning of all real love (Eph. 3:18–19). He commanded believers to seek peace and love (Col. 3:12–15). Yet He was also one tough customer, with justice, truth, and virtue as His goal. His primary message was "Repent, for the kingdom of heaven is at hand" (Matt. 4:17). He accused the leaders of Judaism, the scribes and Pharisees, of being hypocrites (Matt. 23) and declared them a brood of vipers (Matt. 12:34). He condemned in advance any community that would refuse to hear the preaching of the gospel by His disciples, saying it would "be more tolerable for Sodom and Gomorrah in the day of judgment than for that city" (Matt. 10:14, 15; Mark 6:11).

He will ultimately be each person's judge (John 5:21, 22). Christ Himself defined the "exclusivity" of the Christian faith, when He said, "I am the way, the truth, and the life. No one comes to the Father except through Me" (John 14:6). Yet no one who chooses to confess sin, repent, and believe in this Savior is excluded from access to Him (John 3:16).

Christ said that His true followers would not always be honored but would be "hated by all nations for My name's sake" (Matt. 24:9). He said that the world "hates Me because I testify of it that its works are evil" (John 7:7).

Since Christ has been since "the beginning," He was fully present as part of the divine Godhead in the Garden of Eden at the fall of mankind. "Let Us make man in Our image," notes Genesis 1:26, referring to the Trinitarian nature of God. Christ fully understood that humans are not basically good, and, without God, always gravitate toward selfishness and sin (Jer. 17:9; Ps. 14:1; Rom. 3:23). He also knew that, unlike modern psychology claims, humans do not need more self-esteem, but more humility, and that, in fact, the only real peace and security comes from acknowledging our sinfulness before God and inviting Christ into our lives. This decision cannot be forced, but God gives the free will to choose Christ—or reject Him— to every person. Yet it is the duty of every Christian to tell people about the gospel so as many as possible know about this option (Matt. 28:18–20).

As part of the Trinity, Christ witnessed the giving of the Ten Commandments and other laws in the Old Testament. This includes the first commandment: "I am the Lord your God. . . . You shall have no other gods before Me" (Exod. 20:2, 3). Forbidden were the practices of false faith: witchcraft, sorcery, divination (fortune-telling), consulting mediums, calling on the dead, and worshipping or praying to false gods and idols (Deut. 18:10–12; Exod. 22:18; Lev. 19:26, 31; 20:6; 1 Sam. 15:23; 2 Kings 21). The New Testament echoes the same (Acts 16:16–18; 19:11–20; 1 Cor. 10:19–21; Gal. 5:19: 1 Tim. 4:1; Rev. 9:20–21; 21:8; and 22:15).

He was fully present when the ancient nation of Israel, after being led by God out of Egyptian slavery into the promised land of Canaan, deliberately turned to the worship of false gods and goddesses (Isa. 2:6–22; 44:9–20; 45:20; 1 Kings 14; 2 Kings 17, 21; Jer. 7), as well as to sorcery, astrology, and nature worship (Isa. 47:9–13; Jer. 8:2; 2 Kings 21; 2 Chron. 33; Mic. 5:12, 13). Ignoring many divine warnings delivered through the prophets over several hundred years about the consequences of this spiritual unfaithfulness, the Hebrews were eventually conquered by the pagan nations of Assyria and Babylonia.

Christ was well aware of the nature of the spirit world, for He is One with the supreme spirit, the Holy Spirit. The work of the Holy Spirit guided the Old Testament prophets, as well as Christ's direct confrontations with Satan (Matt. 4:1–11; Mark 1:12, 13; Luke 4:1–13). The Holy Spirit has been present and accessible to all true believers in Christ since Christ ascended to heaven and is our spiritual Teacher and Helper, as well as the Spirit of Truth (John 14:16, 17). The Holy Spirit embodies the wisdom of God (1 Cor. 2:10–13) and indwells those who have been "born again" through belief in Christ (John 3:3–5; 1 Pet. 1:3).

Christ, together with God the Father and the Holy Spirit, has power over all things, including Satan (Mark 1:27; Phil. 2:9–11; 1 John 4:4). The demon world is answerable to God (Job 2), and demons tremble before Him (James 2:19). Yet God allows Satan and his army of demons to exist for now, as humans continue to accept Satan's deceptive ideas and temptations, a process begun in the Garden of Eden with the choices Adam and Eve made. Satan saw his own eventual destruction at Christ's resurrection. Still he is committed to a fierce struggle to take as many souls with him as possible (Luke 8:12; Eph. 6:11, 12; 1 Pet. 5:8). All who do not believe in Christ will join Satan in hell for eternity (Matt. 13:31–43; John 3:16). This is a choice people make themselves, by rejecting the free gift of salvation through Christ.

The Reality of the Spiritual Realm

Many churchgoers in America, as well as the other Western nations, are basically secular in their approach to faith, operating as if Christianity is simply a code of values. They have trouble grasping the concept of the omnipotent, present power of God and the existence of an unseen spiritual world, even if they give lip service to it. Or rather, it's easy to accept the *good* spirits—such as angels and, of course, the Holy Spirit—but Satan and demons belong to the category of folklore and myth.

The West is unique in this denial. John P. Newport makes this point in his book, *The New Age Movement and the Biblical Worldview*: "The field of anthropology reveals that throughout Asia, Africa, the Pacific islands, among folk Muslims—virtually anywhere that the Western worldview has not permeated—the idea of evil spirits is an integral part of the worldview of many groups."[1]

Christian missionaries, Newport notes, have encountered difficulties because often they have become so secularized they do not understand how to operate in the spirit realm. In such cases, the casting out of evil spirits ironically continues to be done by local shamans.[2] A truly "multicultural" approach would investigate what these other cultures may understand that Western culture has lost.

Rejecting the dark side of spiritual forces is an arbitrary decision. Of course we would all like to believe that only "good" spirits exist, but what does the evidence show? Christians in particular err in choosing to ignore this aspect of Scripture, for Christ spent a lot of time on this subject. There are thirty-two references in the gospels alone (Matthew, Mark, Luke, and John), where Jesus Himself encounters Satan or demons, or their activities are described.

One doesn't have to become obsessed with exorcism or blame every human ill on demons to accept the truth of spiritual evil as presented in the Bible. C. S. Lewis makes this point eloquently in the preface to *The Screwtape Letters,* when he identifies the two typical approaches to the idea of Satan and demons: either to be overly preoccupied with them or to disbelieve they exist. He explains that both are biblically unsound attitudes.[3]

Christ casts out demons not through ritual, dance, mindless meditation, shouting, wailing, chanting, drumming, praying over certain territories, or other questionable practices that often accompany human endeavors. He exerted authority over them with simple verbal commands (Matt. 8:28–33; Mark 1:27; Luke 4:41). His encounter with Satan in the wilderness (Matt. 4; Mark 1; Luke 4) involved a battle of ideas. Satan verbally assaulted Christ with twisted versions of Scripture, and the incarnate Deity resisted fleshly temptation while correcting Satan's deception, finally calling a halt by reminding him that "It has been said, *'You shall not tempt the Lord your God'"* (Luke 4:12).

Christ's authority and the truth of His word are the essential weapons against the demonic army. Believers are told to pray fervently and arm ourselves with the "full armor of God" (Eph. 6:10–18). This armor includes righteousness, knowledge of God's Word, our salvation promises, a peaceful attitude, and strong faith.

In dealing with the immaterial, certain pagans may have the advantage over many self-labeled Christians. If one has already encountered the spiritual realm, it may be easier to accept the saving faith of Christ and quickly grasp the power of the Holy Spirit.

The Tactics of a Formidable Enemy

Not all people who practice paganism will encounter dark spiritual forces. God is merciful in allowing many who dabble in the occult to fail to make contact with enemy spirits. But these practices are extremely risky because any supernatural encounter made while performing rituals, contacting spirit guides, divination, and the like will not be from the good side of the spirit world—that is, God and/or angelic beings. Since the practitioner is violating God's prohibition against sorcery, his contact will be with deceptive, demonic spirits. This is true regardless of whether the pagan understands this or whether the spirit, if communicating, identifies itself as such.

Classic demonic activity is evident in American life today, especially among "superstar" New Age personalities, some of whom have been embraced by mainline Christians. Mediums who have contact with spirit guides have published best-selling books with their messages. Some masquerade as "Christian" messages. *A Course in Miracles* by psychologist Helen Schucman, published in 1975, has served as the basis for instruction in many Christian churches. It has also been featured on PBS, and there are over a million copies in circulation. Schucman said this material was dictated to her by an inner voice, which identified itself as "Jesus," and said, "This is a course in miracles. Please take notes."[4]

A Course in Miracles is a rambling, nonsensical presentation that uses Christian terminology, even the names of Christ and the Holy Spirit, but radically contradicts scriptural precepts in its ideas. Only a few points are even coherent, and it's a rehash of the ancient deception that we humans are "gods" (or we and God have the same mind). In reality, good and evil do not exist, but are merely false perceptions. The only sin is a lack of the all-encompassing universal "love." Forgiving oneself for pretty much anything is the starting point. There is no punishment, only the correction of this mistake in perception. Grasping this special, secret knowledge will be done only by a few enlightened people. If you do, you are obviously one of the gifted.

Like many counterfeit messages, *Course* has a comforting, prideful, and simple appeal at first reading. People may simply do exactly what they wish and it's okay. Hurting others can be rationalized. Yet the actual result of embracing the *Course* or any similar philosophy is alienation from our real God.

Other spirits have spoken through their human hosts on television for millions to witness. While some are probably fakes, others seem clearly under the influence of an adverse supernatural force. Oprah Winfrey has featured numerous channelers of the occult on her show. On one show, housewife Penny Torres went into a trance to allow a spirit named "Mafu" to speak through her: "Suddenly she begins to shudder, her neck stiffens, her face contorts, and Mafu emerges with a low, growling noise. . . . Mafu takes questions from the audience. . . . His principal message comes through loud and clear: 'That which you humans call God is really within each one of you.'"[5] Amazing—it's the same message that *A Course in Miracles* delivers.

Self-proclaimed medium John Edward in the popular television show *Crossing Over* lends enormous credibility to the occult. Edward has done "readings" for celebrities Roma Downey of *Touched by an Angel*, author Anne Rice, and talk show host Ricki Lake to ostensibly contact deceased relatives.[6]

Apart from such examples of overt demonic activity, the work of Satan and his army of fallen angels has generally been more subtle, as was mentioned in chapter 2. Spirits are intelligent and smoothly manipulate the motivations and ideas of people. Exactly how this is done is not explained in Scripture, and it's probably a good thing. Humans would become paranoid rather quickly and too focused on every thought process or emotion, in an effort to prevail through human willpower. Instead, a person's best defense is knowledge of Scripture and a close relationship with God. A Christian can confidently rely on the power of the Holy Spirit in the ongoing spiritual battle.

All people have souls that will live eternally either in heaven or hell, depending on one's belief (or disbelief) in Christ, rather than one's love of worldliness and evil (John 3:18–21). A person is individually responsible for the sins he or she commits (James 1:12–15), even if demonic forces influence one's life, because a person is fully able to resist Satan through the power available in Christ's name (James 4:7–10).

The primary goal of Satan is to separate human souls eternally from God. As the master of pride (Isa. 14:12–15), he abandoned allegiance to God because of belief in his own abilities (Ezek. 28:12–19). Winning souls to his side is part of his contention with the Almighty.

The tactics of Satan can be low key, if that's all it takes to keep someone from God, or they can be strong and overwhelming. They take the form of deception, dissension, distraction, or destruction, as covered in chapter 2. Satan is the father of lies and murder (John 8:44). He tempted Eve and Adam in the Garden through appeals to their pride so they could believe the lie that they could be like God (Ezek. 28:12–17; Gen. 3:4, 5).

The secular narcissism of American culture and its delusion that Satan doesn't exist has been exploited by dark powers to the hilt. Satan hides "in plain sight" while evidence of demonic influence is everywhere, from simple blind pride to increased psychiatric visits and anxiety disorders, to youth rebellion, and moral and civil chaos on many fronts. Yet most of the intellectual, political, and even religious elite discount the biblical model describing the spirit world.

Satan's seduction can look like something beautiful, noble, or intensely exciting. "For Satan himself transforms himself into an angel of light" (2 Cor. 11:14). Elizabeth Hillstrom notes in *Testing the Spirits* concerning current New Age spiritualism: "[It] . . . acknowledges the existence of other spirit beings . . . and tacitly assumes these beings are good and have our best interests at heart. In strong contradiction to the Bible (see Deut. 18:9–13), it assumes that contacting these spirits, interacting with them, and heeding their advice is a beneficial thing to do."[7]

Yet nothing is beneficial from the demonic realm, and Scripture says to use God's wisdom and protective measures to discern deceiving spirits and overcome them. This is why a Christian is told to "test the spirits." The test is as follows: "By this you know the Spirit of God: Every spirit that confesses that Jesus Christ has come in the flesh is of God, and every spirit that does not confess that Jesus Christ has come in the flesh is not of God" (1 John 4:2, 3). Acknowledging the reality that Christ came to earth is a critical element separating false from real faith.

If the mind is engaged and dwells on truth, it will likely gravitate toward Christ, who is the cornerstone of all truth. Many people know the familiar verse, "You shall know the truth, and the truth shall make you free" (John 8:32). But the verses before and after tell how Christ defines truth: "If you abide in My word, you are My disciples indeed. And you shall know the truth, and the truth shall make you free" (John 8:31, 32). It is His Word that outlines truth. Freedom means being free from the bondage of sin. "Whoever commits sin is a slave of sin" (John 8:34). It is Christ, not the individual human, who defines what sin is through His Word.

Because Christ embodies truth and has authority over deceiving spirits, He is the One who is feared and resisted by followers of false faith, even if they do not understand this is their motivation. The experience of one former witch relates this supremacy of Christ even among witches. A casual Christian, she did not have enough depth in Christian doctrine to understand the danger of spirit beings. She believed she could blend Christianity with witchcraft and ritual involving goddesses and other gods. She incorporated Christ into many of her practices, even using Him to "cast" her witchcraft circle. As she moved up through the hierarchy of the "craft," this became an obstacle:

> Having heard about Christ when I was a child, there were things that stuck to me. I was starting to get very interested in it again. By then it was causing more problems within my group, within my higher-ups in the craft. . . . I asked them, "What's wrong with one Christian God amongst all the pagan gods?" . . . And they just had no answers for me. They just said, "No, you are forbidden to use Christ."[8]

Demons are answerable to Christ, so the real Christ is not readily welcome in pagan ceremonies.

One Christian precept builds upon another, and together they make a very solid and truly enlightening faith, one that transforms the mind. Once that happens, God can effect in each of us seemingly impossible alterations (Rom. 12:2; 2 Cor. 5:16, 17). But this new creation is made by the Creator Himself, so why would one expect anything less?

The Confusion of Religious Syncretism

When people adopt pagan beliefs, they embrace the world in ethereal form. Seemingly progressive yet elemental and primitive, pagan philosophy and practices appeal to fantasy, vanity, beauty, and desire. False gods and goddesses promise unlimited exploration of spiritual and human power, relationships, and sensuality. By contrast, the way of Christ may appear dull and limiting.

Appearances are often deceiving. "I am the bread of life. He who comes to Me shall never hunger, and he who believes in Me shall never thirst" (John 6:35). Even those who choose other roads sense Christ's real power and life-giving qualities. The danger in Christian America is syncretism, thinking one can have it both ways, Christ plus paganism. This "value-added" package is being sold to many youth today who do not know the real cost.

Books, Web sites, television programs about paganism, and even some "Christian" churches weave a deceptive picture for young people about how witchcraft practices can fit into their lives, even that it can amend Christian faith. In the book *Teen Witch* by Silver Ravenwolf, curious teens are told "You do not have to give up your current religion to investigate witchcraft" (23). She tells kids, "Witches celebrate God through religious services, commonly called rituals" (5).[9] Through such misleading messages, added to what schools and the culture already teach regarding "tolerance," many semi-churched or unchurched youth see no danger and are thereby drawn into the blasphemy of sorcery.

In reality, paganism is totally incompatible with Christianity. As a belief system, it justifies violating many, if not all, of the Ten Commandments of the Bible, beginning with the first commandment: "You shall have no other gods before Me" (Exod. 20:3). The prohibition against bowing before carved images or "idols" is frequently ignored (commandment two, Exod. 20:4). Statues of goddesses such as Isis, Diana, Athena, and others are often recommended for pagan altars. Taking the Lord's name in vain is not a problem for most neopagans (commandment three, Exod. 20:7), and the Sabbath day (commandment four, Exod. 20:8) is just like any other day to pagans, who celebrate their own earth-based solstices, equinoxes, and Sabbats. If pagans honor their fathers and mothers (commandment five, Exod. 20:12), it is by choice, since paganism often advocates that children question authority at an early age.

Pagans frequently don't have a problem with adultery (commandment seven, Exod. 20:14), which is any sexual behavior outside of marriage. Bearing false witness (lying—commandment nine, Exod. 20:16) isn't a big deal under the right circumstances, especially to one's parents if they don't approve of occult beliefs. The tenth commandment, which forbids coveting, or envying, someone else's property, personal gifts, or relationships (Exod. 20:17), is often tossed aside like any other boundary. Empowered young pagans are urged to pursue their desires.

In addition to these pillars of the Christian faith, the detailed directives supporting the Ten Commandments are also routinely and enthusiastically broken through profane pagan practices. As mentioned earlier, the Old Testament is full of warnings against all the creative ways humans devised to violate the first commandment. Ancient worship of false gods included practicing sorcery (contacting spirits through ritual, trance, and the like); attempting to foresee the future (divination) through means such as astrology; attempting to manipulate one's future (through the use of charms, potions, or other means); fertility rites involving temple prostitution and worshipping phallic symbols; and attempting to contact the dead through séances or possession by a spirit. Actually, demons pose as dead relatives to deceive the unwary.

These practices are forbidden because God doesn't interact with His followers using these methods. Prophets of God do foretell the future, but the visions, dreams, and messages are always initiated by God and not the prophet. An authentic contact from God will never communicate anything that violates what He has already communicated in His Word (Scripture) and His commandments. There is no need to conduct any ritual as such to get God's attention. It's a good bet that many of God's chosen prophets often wished God would leave them alone, for the path of following Him and delivering His messages was usually a solitary and difficult one.

Another reason these practices are forbidden is that they arise from the individual's need to know something *now*. The pagan mind has a frenzied desire to control situations rather than trusting God to reveal His plans on His timetable under His direction. Since God prohibits such practices, any attempt to make supernatural contact along these lines will not put one in touch with God, but instead one or more demons will mimic whatever the human wants. Demons have personalities and can take on human qualities; they can vary voices, languages, and accents; and it is believed they even have some limited knowledge about future events. All combine to fool the person into believing contact has been made with "God," an "Ascended Master" (an occult spirit identity), the deceased Eleanor Roosevelt, Uncle Albert, or even a self-named "Jesus" who will deliver very un-Jesus-like messages.

By contrast, true believers in Christ do have instant access supernaturally to God through Christian prayer. Just to clarify, the term "prayer" is tossed about casually today, and much praying that is undertaken may not reach the ears of the Almighty. If one prays and has in mind a deity that has qualities other than Jesus Christ or Almighty God as described in Scripture, there's an excellent chance it is falling on deaf ears, or worse, being intercepted by a demonic presence.

How responsive will the true Almighty God be to the young pagan who has been incorrectly told that she can pray to a feminine deity? There is a possibility that the demonic may do whatever possible to "answer" such a prayer request, just to confuse the issue and continue the deception, but in general terms, access to the real Father is not achieved this way. The prophet Isaiah mentions false prayer by the person of compromised faith:

Hear the word of the LORD . . .
"To what purpose is the multitude of your sacrifices to Me?"
Says the LORD . . .
"When you come to appear before Me,
Who has required this from your hand,
To trample My courts? . . .
Your New Moons and appointed feasts
My soul hates;
They are a trouble to Me,
I am weary of bearing them.
When you spread out your hands,
I will hide My eyes from you;
Even though you make many prayers,
I will not hear.
Your hands are full of blood" *(Isa. 1:10–15).*

The New Testament is just as unyielding as the Old Testament in its condemnation of sorcery. In Ephesus, after hearing the preaching of Christ's disciples, "many who believed came confessing and telling their deeds. Also, many of those who had practiced magic brought their books together and burned them in the sight of all" (Acts 19: 18, 19).

In the letter to the Galatians, Paul lists the works of the flesh as "adultery, fornication, uncleanness, lewdness, idolatry, sorcery, hatred, contentions, jealousies, outbursts of wrath, selfish ambitions, dissensions, heresies, envy, murders, drunkenness, revelries, and the like . . . those who practice such things will not inherit the kingdom of God" (Gal. 5:19–21). By contrast, "the fruit of the Spirit [the Holy Spirit] is love, joy, peace, longsuffering, kindness, goodness, faithfulness, gentleness, self-control" (Gal. 5:22, 23).

The element of "self-control" does not mean repression, but instead Christians under the internal direction of the Holy Spirit have knowledge to do what is authentically right and have the liberty to make those choices with this full knowledge. One of Satan's tricks is deception, making sin seem appealing. Believers by contrast can know the whole truth. So they have foresight to understand the consequences, for instance, of adultery—all the people who will be hurt, how ultimately unsatisfying it will be—and because of that are armed with increased information, along with heightened wisdom and good judgment. The Holy Spirit equips each believer, and the extent of knowledge depends on how much the individual deepens his faith through study of Scripture and prayer.

Witchcraft is named in 1 Samuel 15:23 as "rebellion," and idolatry is "stubbornness." Scripture forbids a person to make up their own version of truth, but are to keep their focus on the revealed truth of God: "For the weapons of our warfare are not carnal but mighty in God for pulling down strongholds, casting down arguments and every high thing that exalts itself against the knowledge of God, bringing every thought into captivity to the obedience of Christ" (2 Cor. 10:4, 5).

One of Satan's hallmarks is to plant misleading information in the human mind about who Christ is. Satan works diligently to hide the truly attractive, liberating, life-affirming qualities of a real relationship with Christ, while disguising the bondage that embodies spells, ritual, and invocation of other spirits. The young life that casts aside the Savior and takes up sorcery has traded a "pearl of great price" (Matt. 13:46) for a worthless amulet.

CHAPTER 4

Outreach: How, Why, and Where Paganism Connects with Kids

"Aunt Lenny figured out how to calm me. We would go into the closet in my room and close the door. We'd sit in the dark, cross-legged—in the lotus position—and chant" (*Mercy, Unbound*, 43).

* * *

"There are no coincidences," continued Esmeralda, "only a great deal of magic. . . . If you're born with the talent for magic and don't use it, you'll go insane" (*Magic or Madness*, 263–65).

* * *

"One day, you can be like me," he whispered. . . . "You saw how that girl looked at me? I'm going to have her tonight. I can get any woman I like—or any man, if I was that way inclined. . . . Because I was born with the Power. Power over things seen and unseen. Power over folk and field, power over wind and water. You've got it too, boy" ("The Lightning Bringer," in *Love & Sex: Ten Stories of Truth*, 48).

America's youth are the most privileged, comfortable, and healthy generation in the history of humanity. Why in the world would something dark and pointless like sorcery appeal to them?

If we ascribe to the humanist principle that each person is fundamentally good, this at first makes no sense. With opportunity, money, and physical security, each person should be free to develop his potential to its maximum, and adventures into the spooky and weird just shouldn't be an issue. There would be too much fulfillment with the material world to be tempted by the murkiness of the supernatural.

> *"Now the Spirit expressly says that in latter times some will depart from the faith, giving heed to deceiving spirits and doctrines of demons"* (1 Tim. 4:1).

But wait! What if a "nice" version of paganism was available, one that fits with our world's apparent enlightenment and progress? It's not "black" magic, but "white" witchcraft. It's Glinda the Good Witch, not the Wicked Witch of the West. Surely, this couldn't be harmful, and those who decry it are uninformed alarmists, right?

There is a problem. The biblical view of humanity depicts creatures who, without God, will always drift or race toward self-destruction, especially when destruction looks like paradise. From this view, the puzzle pieces form a very different picture.[1] As America becomes increasingly paganized and stripped of Christian underpinnings, the essence of what can make a person content is changing. Without the taming and softening effect of the gospel, humans descend into mindless self-indulgence, even savagery.

The teens of Columbine, Jonesboro, Pearl (MS), and Paducah weren't desperate inner-city street kids, but middle-class students from small towns or suburbs. The Asian-American who killed students at Virginia Tech wasn't a bum, but a senior English major, whose family lived in suburban Washington. What makes comfortable American kids turn into murderers of fellow classmates?

The heart of a beast is already standard equipment in every child. Honest parents will admit that even toddlers naturally show a viciousness and defiance that cries out for discipline. Kindness and sacrifice do not come naturally to them or to us adults; these are virtues that must be learned. So predictably, if parents begin to tell their children they are their own authorities, they will readily embrace this vision and act accordingly. The supervision of parents and teachers, the authority of the state, and finally the boundaries of God will all be challenged as each attempts to become his/her own "god."

The Purchase of Power

Like most other areas of life, money buys freedom. Our emancipated kids, first and foremost, have cash and know how to spend it. American teens now spend around $190 billion a year, and that figure is expected to grow to $200 billion by 2011.[2] Around 70 percent of teens now have their own cell phones, where they spend about an hour each day talking.[3]

This creates a whole world of influences that are beyond parental control. The publishing industry's preoccupation with the occult in young adult titles instead of earlier themes of sports, pets, and dating, is driven by a market that no longer feels accountable to conventional norms. It is responsive first to youth themselves and their interest in the sensational, and second, to the current parental majority that trusts marketplace values and refuses to demand adherence to traditional standards. The release of the seventh and final Harry Potter book, *Harry Potter and the Deathly Hallows*, illustrates this. Breaking all previous publishing records, the book sold 8.3 million copies in the United States the first day.[4]

To be fair, some parents are alarmed at the new lack of boundaries but don't know what to do about it. Others aren't that concerned, having been indoctrinated to believe humans will gravitate toward what is positive if given an array of options. So, letting a child's eye roam the culture is believed to be safe, and constant vigilance and screening is to be avoided because that would connote "censorship." Only the ignorant, unenlightened, and fearful stoop to such methods.

There's a new term for today's out-of-control youth: "Indigo children." Doreen Virtue, PhD, who writes about them, *approves* of their attributes. Many of these kids, she feels, are mislabeled ADD or ADHD, and instead of giving them medication, she believes parents should just let them be as they are, since they have arrived on this planet to usher in a New Age of peace and have probably lived past lives. The term "indigo" comes from the color of the "aura" that she believes surrounds them.

Virtue describes Indigo children: they feel like royalty and act like it; they feel they deserve to be here; they are confident and often boss their parents around; they have difficulty with authority; they refuse to do certain things; they are creative and often want to "change the system"; they are often loners and have trouble socially at school. Such traits need to be "nurtured" rather than subdued, says Virtue, who gives workshops and speaks frequently to parent groups.[5]

Openly pagan parenting ideas such as these are taken seriously in today's de-Christianized America. Parents may heed such wacky notions, only to collapse in frustration at the inevitable child-rearing crises. How do you fix the child who won't listen, insists on his own way, will behave only when entertained every minute, and is unhappy unless granted the trendiest toy, game, book, or fashion? Children are not aided by unsupervised exploration, but by parents who know there are bad things out there, as well as selfish instincts, and that children need our guidance.

In addition, the consistent act of acquiring develops in kids a habit of greed and self-indulgence, as well as the potential for abuse. Why take care of or cherish anything if there's a replacement toy or a more current electronic gadget available tomorrow? This attitude extends to relationships and people. Everything is now disposable.

How can a parent encourage noble character traits that, coincidentally, arise from the work of the Holy Spirit in a person's life—such as love, joy, peace, longsuffering, kindness, goodness, faithfulness, gentleness, and self-control (Gal. 5:22–23)? Pagan ethics lead one directly away from these qualities, encouraging children to pursue their immediate desires, that is, to read, buy, hear, watch, and experience as much as possible, no matter how outlandish.

The Pagans Next Door

My children don't have pagan influences in their lives, you may be thinking. *We don't know any occultists, Wiccans, or pagans.*

And it's true that openly pagan individuals are a minority. But their presence and influence are growing. Your kids may have neighbors, schoolmates, cousins, and Internet chums who are pagans.

More adults than ever have left all church influence behind and are adopting unorthodox lifestyles. So some pagans and Wiccans are emerging from where you might expect: their unconventional families. Children raised by these Bohemian parents are highly likely to become outright practicing pagans by their teen years. Those who hail from atheist, academic, or intellectual backgrounds are quite comfortable with a pagan identity. The well-educated often spurn a politically incorrect, Bible-based faith yet still seek "spirituality" in some form.

Second- or third-generation pagans are becoming more commonplace. On the networking Web site Witches' Voice (www.witchvox.com), it's not unusual to see youth listings such as this: "My name is Willow, and I've been studying since I was about seven or eight (young, I know, but my grandmother is Wiccan and so are my older sisters). I am thirteen now."

Pagan gatherings are not so secret anymore, and curious youth are often as welcome as adults. Pagan Pride events are held in many cities, and some draw considerable crowds. In North Carolina, an annual Pagan Pride event features a whole array of kid's activities.[6] A southern Minnesota pagan group holds an annual Sacred Harvest Festival, which has a "kid's cauldron."[7] There are even witch camps now for youth.[8]

One young college-age boy writes on his Web site, "I am a Wiccan, duh. I am also gay. . . . My mom set me on my 'New Age' path. I have been reading the Tarot for about six years."[9]

A teen girl writes about how surprised she was at her mom's approval: "She borrowed some of my books, read through them, and approved completely of what my beliefs were, of what I wanted to be. She thought it was good for me and suited me very well. She started to talk about us taking a 'mother-daughter' trip to Salem, Mass. to check out some museums and historical buildings about the Salem Witch Trials."[10]

In certain regions of the country, witchcraft and pagan influences are highly visible. Any child growing up in Salem, Massachusetts, is surrounded by the influences of witchcraft heritage. The Minneapolis-St. Paul area has been nicknamed "Paganistan," and some estimate that 15 percent of the area population is pagan.[11] Unfortunately, some of this occurs within nominally Christian churches.

Llewellyn Publishing, a major publisher of pagan/witchcraft titles, is headquartered in Woodbury, Minnesota, near St. Paul. The company's left-wing pedigree goes back decades to when company president Carl Weschcke was vice president of the Minnesota chapter of the ACLU in 1965.[12] Llewellyn has greatly expanded its offering of youth paperbacks in recent years.

The West Coast is known for its counterculture atmosphere, so it's no surprise that in Seattle, the Fremont area has sizeable solstice and May Day celebrations, including events for kids.[13] In fact, the city of Seattle recently renamed Lincoln Park following a reconstruction project. It is now Solstice Park, because "three pathways leading to a viewpoint overlooking Puget Sound are aligned with the solstices and equinox."[14]

Pagans also now organize youth in ways that are diametrically opposed to Judeo-Christian alternatives. Spiral Scouts was started in 1999 in Seattle as an alternative to the Judeo-Christian focus of the Boy Scouts. Spiral groups are pagan in orientation and tutor kids in occult beliefs and practices.[15]

The boy who sits next to your grandson in social studies may well be immersed in pagan practices at home. More and more of these youth are coming "out of the broom closet" at school. This trend will accelerate as lessons, literature, and class discussions give credibility to a pagan worldview. The presence of openly pagan teachers is also paving the way for students to reveal their beliefs.

School clubs are now a place where the curious youth can explore paganism, sometimes without parental permission or knowledge. Currently, "Anime" clubs and the like are very common in schools. Our local high school in Columbus, Ohio, offers four occult/fantasy extracurricular clubs: the Anime club; a "Magic: The Gathering" club; Dungeons and Dragons; and a Harry Potter club. And a few schools are now allowing openly pagan or witchcraft clubs for students. Among them are public schools in Chantilly, Virginia,[16] and Van Nuys, California.[17]

The ACLU has gotten involved. In 2000 and 2002, students at high schools in Virginia and Texas were asked to remove jewelry adorned with pentagrams, the five-pointed star symbolizing witchcraft, but were allowed to retain them after ACLU intervention.[18] The ACLU also intervened in the case of a girl in Lincoln Park, Michigan, who wore a pentagram necklace to school.[19] School administrators at one time could forbid such symbols because of potential disruption to the school. The entry of well-heeled "religious freedom" legal defense firms into the pagan rights arena is forcing a more radical school climate.

Schooled in Fantasy

How have such ideas taken hold in our schools? Fantasy now dominates most popular youth fiction, television shows, computer games, and movies, so it's no wonder the schools have jumped on board.

Part of the appeal is one of *reconstructing reality.* If you aren't living out all your desires, all you have to do is *envision* a different situation. Hollywood dreams can change Anytown, USA. It might be one reason why Halloween with its costumes and carnival is emerging as our most popular holiday, right behind Christmas. It may also be no accident that Halloween—or Samhain, as witches call it—is the most important annual pagan celebration.

The American social preoccupation with illusion and make-believe brings up serious questions. There is no known precedent of a culture in history where the populace spent a major portion of its time immersed in the imaginary. If you think about it, most American adults probably spend about 20–40 percent of their available waking hours in front of a television show, movie, or at an Internet site. Much of the content is fiction. Throw in our consumption of novels, and it means we are living lives where fantasy is a major player.

On adults this certainly has an impact, but what does this produce in the developing minds and character of today's children? The ability to recognize truth or even want it is becoming less and less.

United States education has wholeheartedly embraced the philosophy that *the best story wins.* Facts and data are increasingly irrelevant. From the whole-language reading method to advocacy-group versions of history, children embrace the imaginary as truth, including their own reflections. Biological and physical science instruction has been transformed by narrow, politically correct notions of environmentalism, with its population control subtext and gloom and doom projections for a revered "Mother Earth."

Literature selections are frequently thinly disguised propaganda as students read stories with an "agenda" that showcase minorities, variant gender roles, deviant behavior, and non-Western spirituality. Much of school-endorsed fiction is composed of graphic, stream-of-consciousness ramblings that seem more like the author's therapy than anything else. And composition exercises from elementary school onward continue the focus on *self,* with a heavy emphasis on journaling. Personal opinion is valued over objective discovery. Journaling may assist writing skills, but often students are given no constructive feedback about content. Instead virtually every thought and feeling is validated.

History classes now dwell disproportionately on oppression, real or imagined, of special interest groups or their subjective utopian dreams: what should be or should have been, from the viewpoint of women, Native Americans, or minorities. While some of this is valid, it often serves another purpose: that of spotlighting, for special antagonism, Western, Christian leadership and values. Our founding fathers are less often heroes to emulate, but instead come off as hypocritical buffoons. The most important "fact" many students learn about Thomas Jefferson is that he supposedly hid a sexual relationship with a slave woman.[20]

Important subjects that should take precious classroom time, according to the National Education Association, now include learning the dates of the gay and lesbian marches on Washington. The NEA also recommends as part of "diversity" instruction to teach students about Diwali, the Hindu festival of lights in October, and about Ramadan, the Islamic holiday in November. For the month of December, however, there is no mention of Christmas.[21]

Further exemplifying this trend away from tradition and toward paganized topics, the Wisconsin Department of Public Instruction's state educational calendar officially recognizes Earth Day in April as Environmental Awareness Day. The department urges schools to use this day to teach about earth concerns. The state education calendar has no mention of Christmas.[22]

Pagan practices are now routine in some schools. Yoga, with all its Eastern religious overtones, is being taught in some districts for student weight management and stress reduction. In December 2006, at a public school in Charlottesville, Virginia, a flyer was distributed, inviting students to a pagan yule observance at a local Unitarian Universalist church.[23] A Detroit charter school, Nataki Talibah Schoolhouse, was featured on the *Today* show because it teaches meditation to its mostly African-American student population.[24]

Reimagining Western Civilization

As political correctness reigns, key historical events are added or eliminated. Schools in Britain recently dropped teaching about the Holocaust and the Crusades because of offense to Islamic students.[25] In the United States, an increasingly disproportionate amount of class time is spent on subjects that distort history. The 1692 Salem witch trials in Massachusetts are a prime example.

While studying early American history, today's grade school student will likely read *Tituba of Salem Village* by Ann Petry, about the Caribbean slave girl implicated in the mayhem in Salem. For many students, a unit on Salem will appear again in middle school. Then in high school, Salem will likely be the focus once more as students read or perform Arthur Miller's play, *The Crucible*. Sometimes classes will also view the 1996 movie starring Wynona Ryder.

Virtually all the material used contains withering portrayals of Christian "fundamentalists" who might dare to believe that Satan exists. The accusers are depicted as irrational, ignorant hypocrites with their own twisted agendas. Tituba and the young Salem girls are often positioned as unwitting victims of bigoted community values that repressed their natural creative gifts and thirst for knowledge.

The takeaway for students is that they have much more to fear from biblical Christianity than from fortune-telling and sorcery, when the reality of the Salem episode is a much more complex illustration of the subject of this book. Satan will use any human weakness to create confusion, to destroy hope in Christ, and to foment dissension, even among believers.

In the Salem trials, the discerning position of Congregational minister Rev. Increase Mather was that "spectral evidence" was not supported by Scripture. Had Mather's advice been heeded, the outcome would have been different. Instead, officials gave credence to the testimonies of accusers who said they had witnessed acts of sorcery by the "spectres" (spirits) of the accused.[26] The Bible's standard for discipline is the testimony of two or more reliable (and living) humans. Faithful adherence to Scripture, rather than being a problem, would have brought sense to the table. In fact, the disastrous episode ended once the warnings of Increase Mather and others were heeded.

The lesson of Salem is not that Satan and sorcery do not exist. It is that, even in the midst of the confusion in which Satan delights, humans owe their allegiance to God and must prayerfully seek careful direction from Him through the Scriptures.

As the influence of paganism grows, "witch persecution" is an increasingly common pop culture theme. It's one of the main topics in

The Da Vinci Code by Dan Brown. It crops up in many teen paperbacks and reruns of *Buffy the Vampire Slayer*. It's a central theme of the Harry Potter books, and it's even the subject of documentaries.

A program on the SciFi cable channel titled "Evil" described witchcraft in positive terms. It's the fastest growing spiritual practice in the United States, the narrator said, and very useful in encouraging "responsibility" among teen girls. The title, though, referred not to witchcraft itself, but to witch hunters, and the program described incident after incident in which suspected witches were allegedly harmed or even killed. This is evidently the real "evil" people should fear.[27]

Planting Deception through Ecology

Many schools are openly delving into alternate spirituality as part of the science curriculum through environmentalism. It is virtually impossible for children to study at any secular school without absorbing the idea that earth deserves nearly godlike reverence. Where did this idea come from? This notion is accompanied by an undisputed ideology that attempts to convince children of the truth of the following statements:

- Humans are destroying the earth, and our population is out of control.
- Animals rank close in importance to humans.
- The earth is sacred.
- Human impulses, being closer to nature, can be trusted.

These assumptions set children up ideally to accept the principles of paganism. It also happens, not coincidentally, that these assumptions are provably false.

Human intelligence and innovation are resources for solving problems, and humans provide labor to accomplish these goals. The earth is nowhere near a "population crisis," and, in fact, population is declining in Europe and hovers at replacement levels in the

United States. While human mistakes have caused environmental damage on a local basis, these are challenges that *human ingenuity* has overcome.

Many experts challenge the implication outlined in school curricula that global disaster is imminent from environmental damage. These so-called experts focus on global warming, food shortages, and overpopulation—all of which is irresponsible and ultimately unsupportable. Yet these one-sided claims are made in school textbooks and environmental curricula disseminated by the federal government through the EPA and the Office of Environmental Education.

One school text reads: "As human activity interferes with the earth's capacity to maintain a maximum range of tolerances for life, history traces the roots of degrading activity to . . . the Judeo-Christian view of humans as having domination over the earth, the industrial and scientific revolutions, and the rise of capitalism."[28]

Some environmental education is quite blatant in teaching kids earth worship. In Port Huron, Michigan, a few years ago, an environmental program for fourth graders called Earthkeepers came under fire from concerned citizens. The activities for children included gathering in a circle, reciting text in unison, and making "magic spots" to contemplate nature. The program's founder was involved with the radical deep ecology movement, which advocates that humans adopt more primitive lifestyles and that population reduction is a necessity in order for nonhuman life to survive.[29]

In a case in Pound Ridge, New York, a U.S. district judge ruled that the Bedford Central School District should halt its programs surrounding Earth Day that essentially constituted religious practices. An altar had been used and third graders had cut out figures of an elephant-headed Hindu god. But a higher court eventually dismissed the suit.[30]

One parent in Ohio wrote to me about a homework assignment from his daughter's fourth grade class. Children were told to choose an animal as part of a "vision quest," which is a Native American occult meditation practice. This parent insisted his daughter be excused from a lesson involving a pagan practice that conflicted with her family's Christian beliefs. Ironically, the parent is part Cherokee.

Classes on multiculturalism routinely incorporate alternate spirituality. Units during the fall often include Halloween themes. Some Spanish language classes feature programs on the "Day of the Dead"—a pagan-based observance from Mexico which occurs around Halloween. And Thanksgiving studies are likely to incorporate elements of Native American nature worship.

Are we to plunge children back into the darkness and bondage of superstition? A key element of pagan-based religions, including witchcraft, maintains that objects and elements of nature have special powers, and that certain rituals performed in very specific ways bring predictable results.

Extremists in the environmental movement believe the earth is sacred. These individuals frequently have spiritual ties to nature religions such as Wicca or goddess worship. Believing that the sun, moon, trees, and animals are imbued with their own spirits that can be contacted and even harnessed by humans is not just a radical idea, but becoming a staple of children's media. The words of the song, "Colors of the Wind" from the movie *Pocahontas*, reflect this concept:

> You think you own whatever land you land on
> The earth is just a dead thing you can claim
> But I know ev'ry rock and tree and creature
> Has a life, has a spirit, has a name.[31]

Superficially it sounds like freedom, but the accompanying ideology is that God is in nature, or that nature is God. This is absolutely contrary to biblical teaching.

This reverence for "earth" is honored on Earth Day. As in the Wisconsin schools previously mentioned, most public schools have some observance on April 22 each year. The Earth Day Network works with more than 105,000 teachers (kindergarten through twelfth grade) in the United States alone.[32]

Enlarging the Web of Deceit

Nature-based concepts resonate with kids and their love for the outdoors. Even for the informed and discerning young American Christian, making sense of these ideas is a challenge, because *confusion* is another characteristic of alternate spirituality. It's also the basis of today's youth culture. Parents are often at a loss to evaluate and understand the world in which their children are growing up because making "no sense" is perfectly acceptable, even celebrated, today. The moral, social, and intellectual free-for-all is disturbing and makes debate difficult.

Where chaos blossoms is on the Internet. Ten-year-olds can talk anonymously to fifty-year-olds and connect in ways that parents may feel is productive—or terrifying. Subjects heretofore forbidden are instantly accessible to the innocent.

Cyberspace is certainly not all bad. Christian material abounds on the Internet. In addition, children are exposed to some harmless and creative whimsy. The boundaries of time, attitude, and language surrender to the non-rules of cyberspace, mixing ancient history and recent technology. Old English dialect juxtaposes with current slang, campy humor, and today's pop icons. My son used to play a user-configured computer game in which Chevrolet Camaros chase Teutonic barons across a medieval landscape.

But another dimension of the Web is irreverence for the sacred. For children this opens up new and dangerous intellectual and spiritual territory. Web sites may seem authoritative, but misinformation and spiritual poison is being transmitted to large audiences in a flash. So ten-year-olds at pagan sites can learn all kinds of creative ways to bypass their parents if they decide to join a coven and engage in rituals.

Occult Internet sites are packed with specific "spells." Pagan youth chat rooms are readily available where youth can talk to teen or adult practitioners and where their fears about these practices can be allayed. *These people seem cool,* the child may think. *Witchcraft can't be all that bad.*

Youth themselves report that the broadest avenue to explore paganism is the Internet. While initially drawn by television shows, games, books, and movies, kids make real connections to overt paganism on the Web. Younger kids go to game and cartoon sites (especially the Japanese "anime" figures), role-playing fantasy sites (such as World of Warcraft and Dungeons and Dragons), and chat rooms for youth on AOL and Yahoo.

But for teens and college students, the real action today is on Facebook, MySpace, Meetup, and other networking sites.

MySpace is dominated by the under-thirty crowd. A search using the term "Wicca" turned up over thirty thousand hits, meaning the word "Wicca" appeared on individual profiles that many times. The term "pagan" yielded over twice as many hits.

Facebook, which caters to the high school and college-age crowd, offers special topic groups under the headings of "paganism/Wicca" as well as "pagan pride." There's also a group for Harry Potter fans, called "Hogwart's School for Witchcraft and Wizardry."

On Meetup.com, youth and adults connect to people with common interests in their city or region. Photos and contact links are included in the postings. An interested person types in a zip code, and up pops covens, pagan groups, and individual Wiccans galore.

Youth listings on WitchVox, the Witches' Voice Web site, are also numerous but have decreased slightly over the past few years (only about thirty-five hundred now, compared to four thousand two years ago). It's most likely because pagan youth are flocking to the larger networking sites. Paganism has definitely gone mainstream.

In an attempt to serve their constituents, Witches' Voice has a forum for teen and college covens to register. A few of these are established community or school clubs; most seem rather informal attempts by one or two teens to start a group. Some are fully functioning covens performing rituals and spells; others are study groups.

Witchcraft becoming stylish is a troubling and serious development. The listings on the pagan Web sites vary widely in gravity. Some teens could be called "bubblegum" witches, simply latching on to a current trend. Others are more serious and identify with narrowly defined pagan or Wiccan "traditions," such as Celtic, Dianic, Druid, Faerie, and Egyptian. Teens who call themselves "Goths" are well represented, as are girls who describe themselves as feminists.

No Fear, No Faith

So dive right in, youth are told. Get rid of your fears. Fear is taboo, unnecessary, and irrelevant because, like the heroine Buffy or the character Yu-Gi, you can always find the power to slay the beast of the moment or satisfy even the most remote desire. Go with your impulses and find the power *within yourself*, just waiting to be discovered. Harnessing that power is the only discipline anyone needs.

But what would unbridled spiritual power be like in the hands of adolescents? What about curses or hexes? Such practices violate the ethics of "real" pagans, according to many in the craft. And adults are evidently supposed to trust kids to stick to the "good" stuff.

Often this power is positioned as "white magic" as opposed to "black magic." In Baltimore, Maryland, in 1998, a ninth-grade girl at Southwestern High School was accused of casting a spell on a classmate, so the principal called the student's mother. The girl's mother is actually her father, now a transsexual Wiccan, who defended her daughter as only practicing benign nature worship.[33]

In 2005, a middle school girl in Michigan wrote the following about witchcraft in her school newspaper:

> My family is a normal family, except that my aunt is a Wiccan witch. . . . I have decided to experiment with this religion and see if this is the way for me. I also think that some of the kids in school would like some of the things that Wiccans do, like: We gather in meetings every week and talk, gossip, and learn about the Wiccan way. We cast spells and potions.

Some parents complained, and school officials promised witchcraft would not be a topic in the paper again.[34]

Adherents assure troubled parents that being a pagan is not dangerous. Yet there are plenty of examples in youth media that belie this portrait of pagan spirituality. Graphic descriptions of raw, undisciplined "magick" abound in teen fiction, many purposely titillating.

The Lightning Bringer, a mysterious character in the teen book, *Love & Sex: Ten Stories of Truth*, offers advice to a boy about harnessing occult power for sexual prowess. This book, on teacher-recommended reading lists for middle and high schools, contains graphic heterosexual and homosexual sex in addition to encounters with the occult. The boy becomes empowered with "lightning" forces to aid his conquest of the girl he craves. The older Lightning Bringer, however, wants her, also, and the boy ends up protecting her from the older man's near-assault. After pages of highly charged eroticism mixed with supernatural events, the story concludes unrealistically as the boy is suddenly tamed by feelings of tenderness for the girl. They stop just short of having sex, perhaps in cooperation with some editor's guidelines.[35]

This seductive potency—the occult combined with sex—fascinates youth and draws them into dangerous, explosive territory. It is an increasingly frequent element in teen fiction. Deriving supernatural power from nature or animals is another popular theme. Coyote, in the Francesca Lia Block book for teens, *Dangerous Angels*, passes down such esoteric "knowledge" to his friend's daughter:

> Coyote was tall. He never smiled. He had chosen to live alone, to work and mourn and see visions, in a nest above the smog. The animals came to him when he spoke their names . . . "I want the horns on your shelf for Angel Juan" Cherokee whispered. . . . Coyote was silent for awhile. Then he spoke . . . "There is power, great power," he said. "You do not understand it yet."[36]

Cherokee's adopted sister, Witch Baby, steals the horns to give to her boyfriend, Angel Juan, so he can gain confidence for the noble goal of performing in their rock band. The horns unleash a dark force that brings enhanced stage presence—including Angel Juan slashing his chest onstage—and eventually leads the group into drinking and drugs. Yet after a "healing ritual" during which Coyote casts the horns into a fire, everything is all right again.[37] Experimentation with the dangerous and forbidden, this lesson demonstrates, has few negative consequences and is actually rewarded. Once again, unleashing powerful unknown forces can always be brought under control; there is really nothing to fear.

The messages are everywhere: there's power to be had, and you can use it for your own purposes. *You* dictate your limits—or lack of them. Harry Potter's desire for revenge on his peers is portrayed as justifiable and seldom discouraged. Po-Ke-Mon and Yu-Gi-Oh cards depicting certain beasts or beings supposedly conjure the "power" needed to compete. What youth isn't drawn to this notion?

In *Shatterglass* by Tamora Pierce, fourteen-year-old Tris is, like many of the characters in current youth fiction, parentless. She is a student of magic at a university, but her inborn powers sometimes get out of control: "They didn't understand that she meditated every day to control her emotions. Without a grip on her temper, Tris didn't just hurt someone's feelings or start a fight. When she lost control, she destroyed property; she sank ships" (93).

When today's American child picks up a book, these are the kinds of explosive ideas implanted in the developing mind. How better to exact "justice" on the bully or tattletale at school? Strong power has great appeal to youth, and if "magick" turns out to be real, kids jump on board for many not-so-great reasons.

Yet this is another cheap cardboard notion that falls apart and leaves our kids helpless, anxious, and insecure when they find out there is indeed much to fear. The bottom-line Christian message is that it's not enough to rely on one's own strength—without Christ in our lives, evil can undo us.

Sadly, one of the most dangerous places for kids to become interested in the occult is today's mainstream chain bookstores, which are packed with occult-themed novels and books for youth. In Columbus, Ohio, a local Borders bookstore advertised a "Sorcerer's School" for Harry Potter fans.[38]

Why is pagan fantasy the fastest growing genre in youth literature? Because it sells, big time. Publishers can flood the market as parents look the other way.

The Vain Imagination of Children's Literature

The nurturing parent needs to exercise great discernment today by monitoring book selections. One of the major entry points into paganism for youth is through novels.

When I was a young teen, I read about Anne of Green Gables, Nancy Drew, and student nurse Sue Barton. Today's girl who shops at Barnes and Noble, Borders, Books-A-Million, Waldenbooks, or B. Dalton's will find no shortage of books about growing up, only now they also incorporate occult practices and themes, sometimes quite shocking. Fantasy is the hottest genre in youth literature.

Younger girls who prefer fantasy are drawn to authors Emily Rodda, Tamora Pierce, Cornelia Funke, Terry Pratchett, P. B. Kerr, Tony DiTerlizzi, and Holly Black. Like Harry Potter, some of these books are wildly clever and very entertaining, yet many include explicit occult elements that may stimulate a stronger interest.

Older teen girls gravitate toward pagan heroines in modern settings with quick reads, such as the Mediator series by Meg Cabot (who also wrote *The Princess Diaries*); books by Margaret Mahy or coven-operator Silver Ravenwolf (who also has her own Web site); the Circle of Three series by Isobel Bird; the Daughters of the Moon series by Lynne Ewing; the Sweep series by Cate Tiernan; and the Magic or Madness series by Justine Larbalestier. Then of course there are countless novelized paperbacks from the television shows *Sabrina: the Teenage Witch*, *Buffy: the Vampire Slayer*, and *Charmed*.

For those who prefer adventure, occult elements are common and becoming bolder. Boys and girls alike read the books of G. P. Taylor, Garth Nix, and Brian Jacques. Adventure, horror, and science fiction appeal to boys, and nowadays blood-and-guts story lines involving demon possession, animal spirits, and human captivity are common. The Cirque du Freak series by Darren Shan features a half-vampire hero working in a circus freak show, punctuated with ample violence and gore.

The novels of Christopher Paolini, *Eragon* and *Eldest*, are fantasies with a Tolkien feel, but the tribal warfare and bloodshed are missing any meaningful redemptive element. They do, however, feature a mind-reading dragon companion for the boy hero.

By far some of the most disturbing books are Phillip Pullman's His Dark Materials series, which include *The Golden Compass*, *The Subtle Knife*, and *The Amber Spyglass*. Pullman presents a creative, semi-modern spiritual journey, but one that is blatantly occult, hostile to God and boldly immerses innocent child characters in harrowing supernatural contests with adult overtones. Whatever happened to the Bobbsey Twins and the Hardy Boys?

Children's media marketers are going berserk trying to satisfy the new curiosity. Many of these books are chockfull of specific instructions and outright tutorials in occult activities and pagan worship. When these heroes or heroines get into a scrape, do they turn to a trusted parent or friend? Do they search their consciences and then do the right thing, even if it's unpopular? Have their consciences been shaped by God—or their own instincts (as with Harry Potter)?

The popular solutions in the new fantasy literature stories are finding power within oneself, contacting the right helper "spirit," or uncovering secret, occult knowledge. Always, the activities are devoid of Christ. Whether it's slaying a dragon or a vampire, getting that A in biology, or even helping out a neighbor, it can be done with the right ritual, a fortune-telling tool, or one's undiscovered powers. No need for "the way, the truth, and the life" (John 14:6).

Reading, Writing, and Ritual

To the extent that they have abandoned the literature classics in favor of these trends, schools and libraries can be some of the most spiritually dangerous places for today's child.

In our community, a private college-preparatory school featured a two-week Harry Potter–themed summer camp several years ago. "Wellington becomes 'School of Wizardry,'" the headline proclaimed in the local paper.[39] Students were to create new Potter characters as they produced a play.

"But Harry Potter gets kids to read!" is the plaintive response to critics. Kids won't read unless the material is occultic? This simply is not true.

But schools seem to believe this myth and are incorporating occultic materials into lesson plans provided by publishing giant, Scholastic Inc. Scholastic sponsors book fairs in many schools at which students and teachers may order from their increasing array of pagan-themed novels, games, and DVDs.

To capitalize on the Potter obsession, Scholastic offers online activities and a discussion forum for kids. Kids are asked, "If you could turn into any animal, what would it be and why?"[40] Scholastic also offers language arts lesson plans in conjunction with *The Golden Compass* book and movie.[41]

In addition to the Potter and Pullman series, Scholastic also publishes Animorphs, whose youth heroes become part-human, part-animal, and have to contend with alien invaders. Scholastic also offers the following series: Gatekeepers, Goosebumps, The Keys to the Kingdom, Remnants, Secrets of Droon, Seventh Tower, Star Wars, T'Witches, The Circle Opens, Everworld, Land of Elyon, and Guardians of Ga'Hoole.[42] To go along with many of the books, the company provides teachers and librarians with teaching material to incorporate into school reading programs.

And Scholastic is not the only entity pushing classroom "magick" with Potter books and their ilk. On the Web are numerous other sites with lesson plans for teachers. One English teacher site has specific lesson outlines for each of the Potter books, including study question and vocabulary worksheets.[43]

The Potter books and other copycats present many false and un-Christian ideas. Defenders will point out that these same wrong-headed notions beckon to youth from numerous Web sites, books, and cartoons, and that's true. But when something has become a worldwide phenomenon, it obviously carries a lot more weight and its flaws need to be quickly enumerated.

The Potter books are fantasy, yet with plot elements that resemble the everyday kid's world: studying—or not; cheating—or not; how to respond to a school bully or a mean teacher; children who take God's name in vain (very ironic, in witchcraft books); making sure one memorizes the names of sorcerers for tomorrow's quiz on "divination."

The cute Potter packaging wraps around some terrifying action, in which children ages eleven through seventeen are faced with life-and-death decisions involving severed limbs, contending with a brotherhood of demons, blood sacrifices, being trapped underwater, the death of a schoolmate, and so on.

But the main problem is the tutoring of children in the principles of authentic pagan myth and occult beliefs. A *USA Today* article featured author Allan Zola Kronzek commenting on the Potter books. "Most of the magic in *Harry Potter* comes out of the Western magical tradition, which really originated in the Middle East, in Babylonia, and Mesopotamia," he said in the interview. Kronzek wrote *The Sorcerer's Companion: A Guide to the Magical World of Harry Potter.* He asserts that these traditions are "where a lot of the magic spells, the potions, and the curses come from."[44]

Yet if your kids are endangered, that's not much comfort. In the same *USA Today* article, I was quoted with my reaction: "From a Christian perspective, sorcery, witchcraft, spell-casting, dealing with the occult has always been forbidden . . . the outcome is that kids are more interested in witchcraft."[45] And young neo-pagans tell us themselves that Harry Potter books are among their favorites.

Since I have been writing about the new paganism and its impact on youth, some Christians tell me they have no problem letting their kids read the Harry Potter series. Denial of the existence of spiritual evil or of Satan has been so ingrained by the secular culture that Christians have lost touch with this reality, even as his fingerprints become more visible.

In the make-believe world of Harry, eleven-year-olds determine "good" and "evil" and go to a school for sorcery—which God calls an "abomination" in Scripture—but many professed followers of Jesus Christ still maintain this is all just harmless fun. There's no *real* danger.

These indifferent Christian parents wave me off, insisting there's really nothing to worry about. And some point to Potter-favorable articles published when the books first became hits: *Christianity Today* (Dec. 13, 1999, and Dec. 28, 2001) and the conservative *Weekly Standard* (Nov. 1, 1999), asserting that Potter is benign and even positive. They compared Potter books to supposedly similar fantasy tales like those of C. S. Lewis.

But I disagree. The Lewis material does not depict children being tutored *positively* in witchcraft and sorcery. When the children in the Narnia tales come into contact with sorcery, it has harmful results. This is a huge distinction. As columnist Roberta Green noted in *World* magazine, "Ms. Rowling has taught children not merely that sorcery exists . . . but that it is good and right to imagine themselves practicing it" (*World*, Jan. 26, 2002).

Yet some parents continue to finance their child's collection of Potter books, along with the wide array of follow-up pagan-themed fiction out there, until the child is old enough to get on the Internet and dialogue with other budding occultists. The only possibility of rescue is if a wise gatekeeper steps into the gap. That gatekeeper used to be the body of Christ, that network of true believers, including the child's parents, guarding the spiritual health and well-being of America's young. What will a child learn from today's Christians?

Doctrines of Demons

If there's one thing I've learned through my catholic education, it's that God is forever forgiving. Perhaps I am on my way to a fiery death under the path that has been chosen for me. However, regardless of the higher power that one chooses to pray to, it is still prayer and someone hears it.

God does not focus on the superficial fact of who or what you choose to worship.

So go the muddled musings of a sixteen-year-old self-proclaimed bisexual Wiccan who attends a Catholic school. This was an e-mail I received in response to an article I wrote about the dangers of teen witchcraft. The gatekeepers have failed this girl, because despite her attendance at a religious school, she didn't understand the basics of the Christian faith, her offense before God, nor the risks of dabbling in the occult.

Kathi Sharpe is a former witch who started a ministry, speaking frequently to youth groups, mostly at traditional churches. She also receives e-mails from many young people and is disturbed at the growing acceptance of the occult. Fifth-, sixth-, and seventh-grade kids who attend Bible-based churches have consulted Ouija boards and organized séances, she reports. One pastor's son reads Harry Potter books and believes there's nothing wrong with them.

How do the parents of these kids react? Sharpe says the parents fall into two categories: either they deny their child's interest in occult activities or they acknowledge them but believe there's little or no risk.

As a former witch, she believes there's great risk. "Harry Potter is about 50 percent fantasy, but the other half is not," she says. The books present real occult practices, terms, and concepts. Her own belief is that Harry Potter books should come with a warning label. After being involved in witchcraft activity for so many years herself, she now takes a firm stance on these books and is particularly concerned about the powerful influence that Scholastic, Inc., the U.S. publisher of the Harry Potter series has within American schools.[46]

The mainline churches are even more questionable. "My church has enjoyed two Wiccan children's directors in the past five years, and Starhawk's prayers and liturgies appear regularly in our order of service." So admits Christine Hoff Kraemer, talking about her mainline church in Austin, Texas. "In my church recently," she continued, "a prominent Austin witch helped lead a service on environmentalism,

an interfaith effort that included music and dance and greatly en-
riched the congregation's understanding of the Earth as Mother."[47]

And if one is tempted to believe this church is an exception among
mainline congregations, guess again. The curious teen who drifts into
a Methodist Cokesbury bookstore or onto its Web site would find
many offerings touting paganism and "feminist spirituality."[48]

Yet there are concerned Methodists fighting this apostasy within
their denomination. The women's Renew Network within United
Methodist churches encourages biblical faithfulness and educates
Methodists, especially women, about the basics of Christianity vs. the
popular heresy within mainline Christianity today.[49]

Meditation practices are becoming popular among mainline
Christian youth groups. Called "contemplative prayer," many Christian teens and parents would be stunned to learn that these same
practices are daily activities of New Agers and pagans.

The Youth Ministry and Spirituality Project (www.ymsp.org) originated at the San Francisco Theological Seminary in 1997 and has
funding from the Lilly Endowment. Participating churches include
Methodists, Presbyterians, United Churches of Christ, Lutheran
(ELCA), and others. The Web site explains why they've gone this direction—to rescue youth groups from fun and games.

What they've gone to instead is what much of the "emerging"
church movement advocates: meditative prayer, ritual, and silence, in
which one listens to the leading of the Spirit. Yet what's frequently
missing is Scripture study, which is how Christians are tutored to recognize the Holy Spirit. Nor is there mention of repentance of sin,
biblically authorized ways to understand God's will, and Christ's
atonement. Marginally informed youth can spend several years in
such groups and have spiritual encounters, entering adulthood believing this was Christianity and that they believe in Jesus. It's no
wonder this "Jesus" may accommodate whatever one wants.

Yet one hears from youth themselves that attendance at a Bible-
believing church is not always an immunization from the seduction
of neo-paganism. One young woman writes about her teen years: "I
am pagan. . . . Five years and a lifetime ago, I was a devoted member

of the Assemblies of God church . . . its youth group, and the Bible Club at my high school." But a family background in the paranormal and sexual interests pulled her away. "I probably would still have been there if . . . a lot of things hadn't happened. If I hadn't fallen in love with a woman. If I hadn't come to the realization, all by myself, that the Divine meant me to be Bisexual."[50]

One insidious element drawing young people toward paganism is the visible "evangelical" Christian left. As wolves in sheep's clothing, they seem appealing because of their tolerant, culturally current approach, even as they claim to be faithful to the Bible's teachings. Yet they are leading youth directly into very un-Christian territory.

Sojourners is a magazine popular with college-age and young adult Christians. Editor Jim Wallis is front and center among the religious left, flanked by popular writers and speakers Tony and Peggy Campolo. They have all compromised seriously over the years by accommodating feminist spirituality, homosexuality, and radical environmentalism—all part of the pagan worldview—as compatible with Christian faith.

Several years back, I was astounded to see the cover article of *Sojourners* feature Miriam Therese Winter, a Catholic feminist and writer of books promoting goddess theology and witchcraft. When I wrote and questioned Jim Wallis for an article I was writing, he replied with a rude, defensive letter. *My* "intolerance" was the problem. Preferring to stick to ad hominem attacks, he never addressed the issue at hand—that Winter's open rejection of God the Father, her interest in witchcraft, and belief in goddesses constitute blasphemy. It just doesn't get any more basic in Christianity than this.[51]

Even celebrity ministers such as Rick Warren have gotten pulled onto the left-wing religious bandwagon. Many of his associates are now the Wallis/Campolo faction, as well as those who espouse support for homosexuality, abortion rights, and contemplative, mystical spirituality.[52]

This is the murky picture of Christianity presented to youth today. Increasingly, biblically faithful Christians are being demonized and marginalized by other self-labeled Christians—and the uninformed, seeking adolescent often finds the lure of the seemingly less restrictive faith irresistible.

Too often today's teens don't see it as an "either/or" choice. They try to mix pagan practices with Christianity. "Isis Rose," an African-American girl whose real name is Avery, talks about her Wiccan friends: "All three of us began training ourselves with the Wiccan basics. You know, calling the spirits, meditation, casting circles, calling the quarters, etc. . . . I still however am involved in Christianity. And everyday I find myself wondering, 'Am I going to hell for this?' 'Does God hate me now?' 'I can't let my parents know.' 'Especially my father.'"[53]

The book *Teen Goddess: How to Look Love & Live Like a Goddess* tells readers that Mary, mother of Jesus, can easily be worshipped as a goddess, and is quick to point out that some "Christian" ministers "pray to a mother-father god rather than just a father god." This will surely relieve the teen girl who has just absorbed in previous pages the misinformation that ancient, peaceful, goddess-worshipping societies were annihilated by the power of the Roman Empire and male-dominated Christianity.[54]

What's the attraction of all this stuff? To kids raised on adrenalin, rebellion spiked with mysticism is the natural next potion. The promise that something supernatural and mysterious might be within a person's grasp breaks the boundaries of youth restraint. *You* can change the world, right from your own bedroom.

And sometimes parents are otherwise occupied. Christian families suffer, unfortunately, from the same traumas and dysfunction as the whole culture. Fathers leave the home or are consumed by work or swallowed up in alcohol, drug, or gambling addictions. Mothers suffer depression, are expected to carry full-time jobs to keep up with the demands of indulgence, or are trapped in their own self-directed sins. It's no wonder children are lonely, sometimes neglected and insecure.

When self-respect is missing from a child's life, alternate spirituality appears to offer a solution. Fantasy weds authority, and even an eleven-year-old orphan nerd like Harry Potter is revealed as a powerful wizard who can excel at sports and take revenge on his enemies. In the lost American child's life, it doesn't get any better than that.

If Satan exists—and if his major goal is to mess with people's minds and spirits to the point where they self-destruct, dismissing the offer of salvation from a merciful Savior—this is exactly how adults and children would be manipulated.

Jesus says, "Whoever causes one of these little ones who believe in Me to sin, it would be better for him if a millstone were hung around his neck and he were drowned in the depth of the sea" (Matt. 18:6).

Hmmm . . .

CHAPTER 5

The Dangers of Living a Pagan Lifestyle

"In this book, we will examine one image of the goddess that is found in many cultures: the young goddess. She is not necessarily a Maiden or virgin, for she may have engaged in sexual activity, by her own initiative or without her consent. Her age varies: sometimes she is ten, sometimes fifteen, sometimes, twenty. She usually lives with her family, but sometimes she is alone in the wilderness." (*Wild Girls: The Path of the Young Goddess,* xv)

*   *   *

"Harking back to the fashions of ancient Crete and Egypt, bare breasts are slowly leaving the beaches and making their comeback into contemporary life." (*Return of the Tribal: A Celebration of Body Adornment,* 3)

*   *   *

"A letter to Cassie from her best friend Mona (not her real name) opened with several lines of unprintable sex talk and ninth-grade gossip, and went on to discuss a teacher. . . . 'Want to help me murder her? She called my parents and told them about my F.' The letter ended with a reminder about a 'neat spell,' drawings of knives and vampire teeth, mushrooms, and a caricature of Mrs. R. lying in a pool of blood." (Columbine victim Cassie Bernall's mom, Misty, writing about her daughter's earlier dabbling in witchcraft, in *She Said Yes*, 38)

Warning: Mature content

The spiritual deception of paganism leads humans into mistakes of a more earthly kind. The Bible says that there is a blindness that accompanies unbelief, especially heightened when the dark powers of evil are involved. "But even if our gospel is veiled, it is veiled to those who are perishing, whose minds the god of this age has blinded" (2 Cor. 4:3, 4).

It's not surprising, then, to find that people involved in paganism are often drawn to lifestyles that are worldly, unproductive, even destructive. What is amazing is the extent to which neo-pagans not only participate in hedonism and rebellion, but also celebrate and embrace it, ignoring, or perhaps unable to see, the hazards. Yet history is littered with lives wrecked by these lifestyles that ultimately bring brokenness and despair.

Fuzzy Brains

One of the first things I noticed when I became a Christian was the new clarity of thought that faith bestowed upon me. Things I had not understood before suddenly came into focus. I also found myself freer from worries and anxieties than in the past. Second Timothy 1:7 turned out to have a deep and abiding meaning for me: "For God has not given us a spirit of fear, but of power and of love and of a sound mind."

By contrast, discussions with pagans young and old reveal hostile prejudices, rigid responses, irrational worries, and circular arguments—even as they believe themselves to be open-minded. Sadly, they seem trapped in futile emotional and ideological patterns. In them, I often see my pre-Christian self, wearily swimming upstream emotionally and mentally without understanding I was doing so.

Elizabeth Hillstrom in *Testing the Spirits* says that nonrational thought is a hallmark of New Age spirituality: "According to New Age thought, messages from the Higher Self can still break through into normal consciousness from time to time . . . as sudden intuitions, insights, profound feelings . . . They do not come through logic or reasoning."[1]

"Go with your feelings" is the message. In *Wild Girls: The Path of the Young Goddess*, Patricia Monaghan outlines a "protective" ritual to heal pain. The young goddess is to visualize a globe of light enveloping her: "Imagine it forming an invisible barrier between yourself and the world. . . . Within that globe you are safe and whole. . . . Whatever emotions come forth, accept them. They are not unspiritual and wrong; they just are."[2]

So today's young neo-pagan has been brainwashed into trusting misleading information combined with gut feelings and desires. Truth and logic are to be distrusted as tools of patriarchal oppression. Recoiling at any suggestion that paganism and its anarchist affinities might be less than beneficial, the pagan gets defensive when confronted with facts that they dismiss as irrelevant or as a power play. This denial is frustrating and makes no sense until one understands that spiritually dark powers, combined with human sinfulness, keep young pagans swirling in blindness and confusion.

A person's instincts, without the discipline of the mind of Christ, with its truth, patience, light, charity, and self-control, usually lead into treacherous territory. Impulsively diving into sensual and irrational experiences is a hallmark of tribal cultures, but also characterizes twenty-first-century affluent American youth.

Young, Dark, and Damaged

Judeo-Christian morality, our offspring are being told, is repressive. Freedom is what a person deserves, and that comes only by listening to one's "heart." The anatomy of today's youth is such that the "heart" shifts frequently from the stomach to the eyes to the adrenal glands, and finally, to the genitals.

It's true that many of the children and teens who gravitate toward neo-paganism are those who are hurting and vulnerable. These are often the students with family struggles, poor peer relationships, or low scholastic achievement. But the attraction of outlaw spirituality isn't always the result of misfortune. Perhaps just as frequently, the culprit is just plain old boredom or bad influences. And bad influences abound in today's America.

The explosion in "body modification" exemplifies the trend. A young man on a very explicit Web site about piercing and cutting reveals his perspective, that it was "youth's way of reclaiming all of our heritage as a tribal culture." He first became interested at a Lollapalooza rock concert, where he visited a booth to have his nostrils pierced. He viewed this as "enlightenment and awareness" of what it means to be a human being. After studying Native American culture and shamanism, he then had his ears stretched and now places coyote teeth in his ear lobes. His spiritual perspective has evolved as well. He has gained "some insight into what bod mod means to the planet Gaiea and her peoples. As for me, I plan on continuing this quest on this planet and in this life and beyond."[3]

Many believe the "body modification" trend indicates a regression to tribal pagan practices. Not every person who pierces or scars himself embraces sorcery, but those involved in the occult have driven the fashion trend. Some "piercees" even see the process as part of a religious ritual of healing and "truth." Deliberately seeking pain is the objective.[4]

What makes beautiful, healthy, young people do such things to themselves, believing not only that it's not abnormal, but also that it's a positive experience and an attractive look? Rev. Steve Schlissel of Brooklyn, New York, has a theory about the motivation. "The fundamental need of fallen man is *atonement*," he writes. Yet the pagan approach fails to achieve the goal. "There is only one God-provided atonement, and that is the pierced and risen Christ," Schlissel explains.[5]

The book *She Said Yes* contains a mother's bittersweet memories of both the bad and good times in her teen daughter's life. Cassie Bernall was the seventeen-year-old who, when asked by one of the Columbine killers if she believed in God, answered affirmatively. She paid for that answer with her life when he pointed a gun at her head and fired at close range.

Misty Bernall writes about Cassie's strong faith in Christ, her poetry celebrating a relationship with Him, and the precious Bible she always carried. But Cassie's life hadn't always centered on hope in God. Her early teen years, her mother writes, were dark and disturbing. Under the sway of wayward friends, she had dabbled in witchcraft, Satanism, and substance abuse, and had even considered violent acts against her parents and teachers.

When they realized the gravity of the situation, Misty and her husband transferred Cassie to another school and severed the questionable friendships. They insisted she attend a Christian youth group, and she initially responded by becoming sullen and rebellious. But little by little the message penetrated Cassie's heart, and they saw amazing changes in her life.

Cassie wrote later in her journal, reflecting on her earlier struggles: "I cannot explain in words how much I hurt. I didn't know how to deal with this hurt, so I physically hurt myself. . . . Thoughts of suicide obsessed me for days, but I was too frightened to actually do it, so I 'compromised' by scratching my hands and wrists with a sharp metal file until I bled . . . I still have scars."[6]

Witchcraft beliefs played a role in the double suicide of two thirteen-year-old girls in Indiana in 2004, authorities discovered, after they intentionally walked into the path of an oncoming train. The girls left notes for their families stating their intentions to end their lives, conveying the belief they would be reincarnated, and indicating that their decision involved witchcraft.[7]

Does everyone who's involved in witchcraft contemplate suicide, get pierced and tattooed, and cut themselves? That would, of course, be a gross generalization. But parents whose children are drawn to "magick" and occult subject matter need to know that such practices are particularly prevalent among pagan youth.

Writers of hot-selling youth fiction know this and include much about pagan styles and practices, which are usually portrayed as hip, cool, and consequence-free, as the following excerpt shows: "Serena Killingsworth walked toward them. . . . Her short hair, currently colored Crayola-red, was twisted into bobby-pin curls. A nose ring glistened on the side of her nose. She wore purple lipstick, red-brown eye shadow . . . Serena stuck out her pierced tongue, showing off the stainless-steel barbell."[8]

The alternate lifestyles adopted by those drawn to the occult take them into a netherworld of bizarre tastes, fashion, entertainment, and behavior. At an age when the blush of youth should glory in natural beauty and reflect warmth, health, and vibrant hues, these kids often don unnatural neon colors for hair and clothing. Preoccupied with the costumes and environments of death and dying, they often obsess on nighttime and darkness. Their ideal becomes dim, smoky clubs populated by drab figures whose only color may be orange hair or blood-red lipstick on a pasty, white face.

One young lady on the Witches' Voice Web site describes her style: "I may dress in mainly black, wear baggy jeans, and have too much black eye liner on, but that doesn't mean I won't befriend a person who is the most popular person in school." She also says she's bisexual.

Retail has caught on to the trend. The clothing at "Hot Topic" (www.hottopic.com) popularizes the "Goth" style. Skimpy T-shirts for girls, oversized black jeans for guys, "bondage" jewelry and accessories, and pentagrams beckon the young pagan ready to spend Mom's or Dad's cash.

Illusion is preferred over reality, and dreams over truth. But even the dreams are the stuff of nightmares. In the marginally incoherent teen paperback *Girl Goddess # 9*, two girls start a magazine and land a backstage interview with their idol, a pop star named Nick Agate.

The concert was sincerely awe-weaving and mind-unraveling . . . there were jugglers, panthers, acrobats, naked children with wings, dwarves, a white horse, swine . . . best of all nick agate he came dancing out on stilts wearing a devil mask . . . he pretended to do it with this ghost-type-thing. he stripped off his clothes and dove into a pit of fire. he sang prince of fire consume me.[9]

Chaos, depravity, and blasphemy are the styles, supposedly expressing boundless confidence and creativity. Are derangement and vulgarity the goals we have for our kids? *Girl Goddess #9* is a collection of short stories by the popular author of youth fiction, Francesca Lia Block. Other stories in the collection feature a pubescent girl whose mother just committed suicide and whose father is drowning his sorrows in a bottle; a girl who lives with her mother and the woman's lesbian lover, whom she later discovers is really her father who underwent a sex-change operation; and a young man's memories about a girl he knew in high school who slept with rock stars and then overdosed on heroin.

Dark powers and pagan beliefs are interwoven into virtually every story. It's the kind of subject matter that's alluring to teens in a train-wreck/melodrama kind of way.

But it doesn't end at fiction. Outright tribalism is one clear manifestation of the trend, showing up in ritualized events. First held in San Francisco, now in the Nevada desert, the "Burning Man" event attracts forty-eight thousand participants, mostly youth, who create a pagan city over Labor Day weekend. Amid exhibits of avant garde art and sculpture are drumming, drugs, chaotic music, and sexual abandon. There are no rules, except the most minimal to ensure safety. The climax is the burning of a gigantic person figure in a rite of simulated pagan worship. Many of the college students who attend just come for the whimsy and abandon, but its pagan roots are taken quite seriously by others.[10]

Valley Girl/Cosmo-Witch

The black-clad raver with rainbow hair may be one common pagan style, but a totally different trend is simultaneously emerging. Following the popularity of television shows such as *Charmed* and *Buffy the Vampire Slayer*, the media is offering a spiffed-up, more mainstream neo-pagan profile. Girls especially are signing on.

"I'm 15 and on the varsity cheerleading squad and swim/diving team," writes a girl from St. Louis on the Witches' Voice Web site. "My family is Catholic except for my aunt who is a priestess . . . we are both studying the celtic/irish/Scottish path." Attractive, accomplished, self-confident, a good student with supportive parents—this is the new American teen pagan.

Camryn Barnes, one of the twins in Scholastic Inc.'s book series, "T'Witches," exemplifies the new image. Her sister Alex, the more counterculture sibling, calls her "MTV girl." Cam is the new Wiccan—pretty, popular, fashion-conscious, pursued by the star of the basketball team—just the role model many parents would choose for their daughters. Television's Sabrina, scrubbed-cheeked and harmless, fits the prototype as well.

The *Charmed* trio of savvy sisters (Phoebe, Piper, and Paige), Buffy, and other witch pop-heroines are a sophisticated next step: confident, sexually active, lipstick feminists who don't take any guff from vampires, demons, or the guy at work. Empowered to remake the world in their own image, these girls use divination, ritual, spell books, charms, potions, and any earthly or supernatural trick the scriptwriters can conjure. Through it all, the hair, nails, and clothes remain flawless and to die for. The male witch characters are appropriately gorgeous but subdued and egalitarian. Only the evil males (i.e.,"bad" witches) exhibit evidence of adequate testosterone.

This new "Cosmo-craft" fusion brings with it a value system that most Christian parents abhor. Makeup, trendy fashions, and physical attractiveness are paramount, as is getting your own way. These are "good" pagan youth who have "ethics"—although they make them up on the run. They are emancipated early from permissive parents, formal education is kind of iffy, and financial support comes from out of the blue.

A good example of this is the site of the Web magazine *New Witch* (www.newwitch.com). Stylish and hip, brash and opinionated, this is young pagan feminism at its most revealing. Humility, tradition, and modesty are not welcome—and neither are authentic Christians.

In the world of the young pagan, the sexual subtext is everywhere. Premarital sex is wedded in an unholy alliance to an alluring, if false, faith. Acceptance of homosexuality and bisexuality is a given; even kinky sexual practices surface from time to time. And the "safe sex" and proabortion sympathies are taken for granted. There is truly no other viewpoint.

In the popular teen book, *Peeps*, a young college student tracks vampires all over New York City because he himself is a carrier of the parasite that makes a person "horny." He got it from having sex with one girl; by the end of the book, he is having sex with another. No discussion of waiting or even of a serious relationship occurs. They have latex; that's all the commitment needed.[11]

Like Barbie with a Book of Shadows and her own condoms, this trend unites the worst of many behaviors. And there are plenty of Web sites helping to cement this foundation. A popular Web site for teen girls is www.gURL.com, started by Primedia Corporation, which also published *Seventeen* magazine before its sale several years back. The site has fashion tips, horoscopes, and "dating" advice, such as "Take the astro-love compatibility test: it's written in the stars!" A recent feature asked the question, "What's your animal spirit? A personality quiz." Another queried, "Do you believe in magic?" And another page has a discussion board all about the occult.

On the site is a huge section called "Sex." On the Sex page are some jaw-dropping discussions and questions, supposedly from girls, that easily qualify as textual pornography. There's also a sprinkling of talk about abstinence, perhaps to subdue parental objections.

"Our content deals frankly with sexuality, emotions, body image, etc.," explains the background section, noting that gURL.com is for ages thirteen and up. A Note to Parents page says essentially that if the material on this site is not what your daughter is "ready" for, "direct her to another site."[12]

Today, wherever you find pagan beliefs, you will find kids being sexualized early, and wherever you find kids being sexualized early, you will likely find paganism. You won't find graphic sex advice columns on a Christian site, because Christians are committed to what's best for youth: the freedom to be innocent during childhood and abstinent until marriage.

Outlaw Sex as a Pagan Right

Among pagans, youth are often told that sexual expression even as a young person is a basic human right and closely aligned with spiritual enlightenment. Starhawk, famous witch writer and speaker, wrote, "We see mutually pleasurable erotic expression in all its diverse forms as a sacred act. We believe all people, including and especially young people, have the right to information about sexuality, health, and sexual responsibility."[13]

To the enlightened like Starhawk, "responsibility" has a new twist. Any "control of sexuality by others . . . is a . . . cornerstone of the structures of domination."[14] The ancient ways that included sexual rites at the pagan temple, she believes, were really the good old days.[15] In earlier times, "sexual identity may have been more fluid." The goddess Inanna was to be admired because she was uninhibited in her sexual appetites and practices and yet was able to keep from getting pregnant.[16] This recent twist on obvious fertility tales reflects the modern pagan obsession with reconstructing truth. "Responsibility," according to Starhawk, means sterility most of the time.

Sex, divorced from fertility, is the platform for sex education classes, and it's at the foundation of paganism as expressed by most of its leaders. Not that babies and children aren't celebrated and appreciated at times. But they are clearly incidental to the vastly more important goal of satisfying one's desires, and they are never to "control" one's destiny.

Paganism marries sex to religious faith and ritual practice. One of the most obvious symptoms of the apostasy of current mainline Christianity is the extent to which outright pagan sexual "values" are quickly being incorporated into church life and beliefs.

One book that has been popular within liberal mainline Christian churches is Thomas Moore's *The Soul of Sex: Cultivating Life as an Act of Love.* A former Catholic monk, now a married psychotherapist, Moore stops short of advocating sex on church altars in imitation of the ancients, but he would celebrate almost everything else. He sees sex as the key to knowing God.

For the ordinary person, Moore believes sex can give one a "taste of eternity."[17] And it should be like a religious experience. "Lovemaking," he writes, "is a ritual that invites the goddess of sex to be present."[18]

Moore spends lots of time talking about phalluses as used in ancient religious rites—how we need to rediscover the religious power of sex and the phallus.[19] Moore recommends that we bring portraits and sculptures of erotic images and gods and goddesses into our homes and gardens.[20] He points out that, for those who are gay, the goddess Diana (Artemis to the Greeks) can be a special patroness because of her androgyny.[21]

To those unfamiliar with the Old Testament, this may seem like breakthrough material, but it's almost a parody of the sins of the ancient Hebrews, who incorporated sexual practices of neighboring pagan cultures into their worship. Prophets Isaiah, Jeremiah, and others repeatedly warned Israel and Judah of the dire consequences of this spiritual "adultery" and its accompanying depraved practices, which eventually included child sacrifice. The record shows, however, that they didn't listen. What followed was conquest and expulsion from the land because of their rebellion. God gave His fickle people a message through Isaiah: "[Y]ou have uncovered yourself to those other than Me . . . You have enlarged your bed and made a covenant with them . . . When you cry out, Let your collection of idols deliver you" (Isa. 57:8, 13).

The young person interested in paganism will not have to wonder long about what sexual ethics pagans espouse. A few visits to high-traffic Web sites of pagan leaders and groups quickly reveals the permissive nature of pagan sexual practices and the kinds of role models they will emulate.

Isaac Bonewits's home page is a good example. He is a prominent pagan and frankly describes himself as "90-percent heterosexual" and "polyamorous." He explains that this "'lovestyle' of intimate relationships with more than one other person at a time, is tied closely to my polytheism."[22]

Sexual Anarchy

The pagan ethic of hedonistic sexuality is neatly packaged and sold to youth in today's social engineering agendas of "reproductive choice" and "gay, lesbian, bisexual, and transgendered (GLBT) rights."

Most of the leaders of the pagan women's movement are vigorously proabortion. Zsuzsuanna Budapest is blunt: "Where does it say that every little soul that manages to land a fertilized egg is entitled to occupancy? . . . The shadow of motherhood is abortion, which is also our responsibility . . ."[23] College students, teens and now even younger children are recipients of these horrific messages.

The ties of these advocacy movements to paganism are very strong. Witch Margot Adler credits much of the development of modern paganism to homosexuals: "Just as the women's spirituality movement received some of its strength, its push, its most dynamic energy from lesbian women, gay men have often been at the forefront of developing this new view of male spirituality."[24] Englishman Alex Sanders, the father of the "Alexandrian" tradition of witchcraft, was bisexual.[25] Leo Martello, considered an "elder" of the craft until his death in 2000, was a gay activist as well as founder of the Witches' Anti-Defamation League.[26]

When I was a socially liberal, twenty-something young woman, I signed on to volunteer at Planned Parenthood. My role was to teach new patients about contraceptives. Tragically, most were teenagers, and, just as tragically, I was enabling them to continue down a wrong road. Mercifully, a job change necessitated my relocation to another town, and, for a variety of reasons, I never re-affiliated with the organization.

This brief stint opened my eyes to several realities of the pro-choice cause. When I applied to become a volunteer, I was asked to fill out a long, detailed questionnaire about my sexual attitudes. The sometimes-graphic questions were intended to elicit appropriately progressive responses. I wondered why this was necessary, if the goal was to keep girls from becoming pregnant. Only years later, as more information has emerged about Planned Parenthood, is the picture clear. As a result of their programs and services, which are provided through a mask of "responsibility," young people are enticed into and kept involved in sexual activity, which inevitably leads many to seek out continuing contraceptives, screening tests for sexually transmitted diseases, and lucrative abortions. Whether this is an organizational goal or just an unintended by-product of their activities is uncertain.

One chilling tale was recently related to me by a friend. She waited outside a committee room at the Ohio House of Representatives one afternoon, hoping to testify in favor of a bill that would outlaw abortion in the state. As she waited, a group of proabortion feminists were gathered, lifting up an invocation to the goddess Isis. The bill did not pass.

If there was ever any doubt that promoters of paganism were cozy with the notion of homosexuality, those doubts were put to rest in October 2007 when J. K. Rowling, author of the Harry Potter books, casually announced that one of the series' major characters was "gay" and had been all along.[27] This pro-homosexual affinity, after millions of children had come to admire the character of Professor Dumbledore, caught parents by surprise. What do Harry Potter–supportive parents, particularly Christians, tell their kids *now*?

The closer a person examines the sexual messages to kids by the paganized spirit of our time, the worse it gets. Some believe the problem is simply an "antifamily" agenda of getting kids to accept heterosexual sex before marriage or homosexuality. There's an even more foundational message aimed at youth, one that threatens their very sanity and selfhood.

Youth are being awakened sexually at younger and younger ages, continuously exposed to stimulating images, and offered "choices" of fluid sexual behaviors, including homosexual activity. Then they are told that even male and female roles, clothing, mannerisms, and biology are changeable if one desires. In short, our kids are growing up to accept and seriously consider an ideal of *androgyny*, a blurring of masculinity and femininity—carried out under a smorgasbord of erotic practices that some call "pansexuality."

Creating the Pagan Pansexual

Psychiatrist Jeffrey Satinover, MD, discusses this as the cornerstone of what we think of as homosexuality:

> Keen observers of the gay scene—many gay themselves— have cogently argued that the gay lifestyle is not so much "homosexual" as "pansexual." And indeed, this observation suggests an important point: that there really may be no such thing as "homosexuality." . . . What we call the "gay lifestyle" is in large measure a way of life constructed around *uncon-strained* sexuality.[28]

There is really no "gay" and "straight" dichotomy in a culture—at least not for long—but, rather, an acceptance of homosexual behaviors leads to complete sexual license, if Dr. Satinover is correct. Scripture leads to the same conclusion, if one looks closely at Genesis 19, Leviticus 18, and elsewhere.

As discussed in chapter 3, the Holy Spirit provides appropriate boundaries for sexual pleasure. Pagan spirits, by contrast, dissolve safe and secure venues, ultimately undermining relationships and diminishing pleasure as well.

Sexual activity apart from procreation—trying mostly to avoid it—is a crucial cornerstone of this new lifestyle. The emphasis is on casual contraception with condoms as a tool of promiscuity, as well as "outercourse," that is, all the various activities that bring sexual stimulation other than intercourse. Those behaviors, our children are taught, can be done alone, or with a peer of the same or opposite sex, even before puberty. At times, it is hinted, they may choose to engage in these activities with an adult.

In the writings of pagan teens on the Internet, whether on the Witches' Voice Web site (www.witchvox.com) or elsewhere, a high number announce their bisexuality, especially girls. A push to label oneself homosexual or bisexual is happening at earlier ages—twelve, thirteen, fourteen—and is being celebrated as the discovery of one's natural urges, rather than the predictable outcome of an incessant propaganda campaign leading toward youth corruption.

Feminist pagan leaders not only tolerate this amorphous promiscuity; they promote it. Philip G. Davis notes that some goddess-worship writers specifically encourage lesbianism and bisexuality.[29]

The boundary-smashing messages of both pansexuality and paganism are everywhere in mainstream youth culture, starting in preschool and elementary grades. One book for young children studying "diversity" is *The Duke Who Outlawed Jellybeans*. In this collection of supposed fairy tales, pagan spirituality, homosexuality, and gender variance abounds. In one story, a little boy named Peter lives with two lesbians, his mother and his mother's friend, who is a sorcerer.[30] This book first came to my attention when a concerned volunteer in a suburban Columbus public library told me one of the librarians was reading it to preschoolers during a regular story time.

Homosexuality is not simply tolerated by pagans, but many prominent pagan spiritual groups foster and support it, even among youth. The Unitarian Universalist church, which embraces pagan ritual and practices, has an office of bisexual, gay, lesbian, and transgender concerns, which actively supports efforts to legalize homosexual marriage.[31] Unitarian Universalist churches are often hosts of local homosexual youth group meetings as well.

Homosexual community groups for youth now exist in most large U.S. cities, inviting middle- and high school–age youth who are interested in homosexuality to drop in and socialize. They operate independently of any school, are often funded by local social service agencies such as United Way, and do not require parental permission or knowledge for young people to attend.[32]

Schools are jumping on the homosexual bandwagon as well. Students may encounter lessons encouraging acceptance of homosexual lifestyles from grade school on. National activist organizations are now well networked within U.S. schools as parents remain silent or unaware. GLSEN, the Gay, Lesbian, and Straight Education Network, has produced some jaw-dropping material for schools and youth. One includes a lesson plan called "Bisexual Basics." The lesson would teach kids that "[e]ach of us should have the freedom to explore our sexual orientation and find our own unique expression of lesbian, bisexual, gay, straight, or *any combination of these*" (emphasis added). This lesson is recommended for students as young as middle school.[33]

This same organization helped produce a brochure called "The Little Black Book," which was distributed to middle and high school students in Massachusetts. It included extremely graphic descriptions and drawings for "queer boys" about so-called safe sex and where to go in Boston to find other homosexuals. The book also urges boys to "come out" early and declare themselves homosexual.[34]

Another group, PFLAG (Parents, Families, and Friends of Lesbians and Gays) has chapters all over the country and many meet in liberal churches. They support gender variance (cross-dressing) even for grade school children.[35]

Their goal is to assist the fragile identities of "GLBT" youth. Far from being considered a renegade organization, PFLAG recently developed a cooperative arrangement with the national PTA.[36] GLSEN's founder and president, Kevin Jennings, who was awarded a special commendation at a recent annual convention of the National Education Association, even has his own page on the NEA Web site explaining his version of "safety" in schools. It includes banning all criticism and opposition to homosexuality, which he and others slickly label as a form of bullying.[37]

Why are so many schools supporting the homosexual agenda, when it is full of high-risk messages for kids? Unfortunately, a growing adult segment of the culture is embracing at least a part of the pagan ethic, and that includes some misguided educators.

Gender Blending and Paganism

"It should come as no surprise that the revival of pagan religion in our day should be accompanied by a stark reappearance of pagan sexuality," Peter Jones, PhD, and Tal Brooke write. A blurring of male and female distinctions is acceptable, even ideal among New Agers like Shirley McLaine, who believe the enlightened person is "androgynous, a perfect balance."[38]

For decades, feminists have been preaching to men and the culture about the need to explore their "feminine" sides, while encouraging women to mimic male assertiveness. Alternate spirituality kicks this up some definite notches into what can be a very weird zone. You can be an Amazon, a male drag queen, or anything in between—all on the same day. Constant change is celebrated, even encouraged.

What's the prognosis for the sexual lifestyle of the teen pagan? It will depend to some extent on the type of paganism attractive to each teen. The major types of witchcraft are Gardnerian, Alexandrian, Celtic, Dianic, Stregherian, Discordian, and Asatru. We'll not be able to cover these in detail here, except for a few comments. The Dianic tradition appeals to lesbians in significant numbers. Some traditions (like Alexandrian) often perform their rituals "sky-clad," or nude.

Another tradition, Faerie Wicca, encompasses overtly sexualized and gender-bending behavior: "Strong emphasis is placed on sensual experience and awareness, including sexual mysticism, which is not limited to heterosexual expression. . . . there is a certain amorality historically associated with the [faerie] Tradition."[39]

This amorality may include pedophilia. The loosely associated Radical Faeries encompass a branch of homosexual activism founded by recently deceased Harry Hay, who was an advocate of "man-boy love,"[40] a term for child molestation.

As paganism goes mainstream, so do these horrific ideas and behaviors. A "transgendered" identity is fast becoming a hotly defended lifestyle right behind homosexuality.

There is a unique connection between sorcerers and "crossdressers" or transsexuals (those who have sex-change hormones or surgery). A tribal tradition that pops up around the globe in both ancient and current times is the cross-dressing witch doctor/shaman, called a *berdache* among American Indians. Biologically, this person is a male, but dressing and living as a female. This "two-spirit" person was considered to have special powers and supernatural gifts.[41] Referring to the *berdache*, Margot Adler says, "it is often easier for someone who is not tied down to specific gender roles to walk between the worlds."[42]

Today's pagan youth who suffers from a gender identity disorder may summon this image when trying to glamorize or justify this path, yet it remains one of confusion and turmoil. And the young person may be reinforced in some schools where the "two-spirit" concept has been introduced during Native American/multicultural studies, even as part of lessons leading up to Thanksgiving.

In the Washington, D.C., area, transgendered individuals were the target audience for several True Spirit conferences held from 2000 to 2003. True Spirit featured workshops on breast removal, hormone therapy, and the social challenges of dressing or reconstructing oneself as the opposite sex. It was a truly horrifying and sad spectacle to which youth were invited. Teen girls sat in rapt attention as plastic surgeons told how they could have their breasts amputated in order to "become" boys.

At True Spirit, workshops also examined sadomasochism as well as polyamory. In keeping with the conference name suggesting a metaphysical origin of this confusion, the conference also offered in 2002 a workshop on "Sacred Body, Sacred Sex" led by a Wiccan priestess.[43]

One is tempted to dismiss such a conference as a goofy fringe element, until one learns that True Spirit was cosponsored by the Human Rights Campaign, the highly influential gay rights lobbying group in Washington. HRC executives are regular guests on national news programs. Then-President Bill Clinton addressed HRC's annual meeting dinner in October 1999. It may not be accepted yet on Main Street, USA, but when it's okay on Pennsylvania Avenue, our kids are surely listening.

The work of True Spirit has recently been absorbed into mainstream national groups such as Gender PAC, whose national conferences have a youth activist training component. It's now an activist issue, this gender-switching. And when kids reach college, they'll be able to "benefit" from the new frontier of co-ed/gender-neutral dormitory rooms. In colleges such as Wesleyan, Haverford, Swarthmore, University of Pennsylvania, and others, a girl and boy can now share the same room. This is called "progress."

The Violent Rainbow's End

There's yet another, more sinister, aspect of this belief system. Despite the protests of many teens who've written me e-mails, there can be little dispute that paganism has a core of wildness that can quickly unleash anger and violence. Not only is this tolerated, but it is at times encouraged and celebrated:

> Like "witch," the term "magic" signifies strength and competence, it tastes of power as it trips across the tongue. Moreover, in its common usage, the power of magic is naked, unbridled power: it is the capability to kill or to heal, to curse or to bless. . . . in the wrong hands, magic could be like a thermonuclear device in the trunk of a terrorist's car.[44]

There is only the pagan's conscience to limit the use of this spiritual device. Unlike Christianity, there is no unchanging ethical system that forbids killing, stealing, lying, coveting, or committing adultery to guide one's behavior. Nor is there an ultimate, omnipotent authority like Almighty God—or so they believe. The human is the authority.

In feminist spirituality, this is embraced. Starhawk says, "The Goddess liberates the energy of our anger. It is seen as sacred, and its power is purified." So the Goddess represents all aspects of nature, and that's okay. She's life and death, love and hate. "She is the bird of the spirit and the sow that eats its own young. . . . She brings both comfort and pain."[45]

Just the kind of information the parent of a newly declared teen pagan wants to hear. In the hands of immature youth, this kind of "permission" is a ticket to disaster. Modern witchcraft does, however, espouse a standard called the Threefold Law, a belief that anything a witch does to another comes back to them at three times the original power.[46] While this may provide a measure of restraint, it can also be discarded if necessary. When there is enough anger, many witches decide they are willing to risk what they believe will be the natural consequences in order to see "justice" done.

The individual is the arbiter of such justice, and each person has her own reality and truth. Dr. Jeffrey Satinover says of paganism: "No single moral standard governs the lives of men, and except by the power of force, no god, and no corresponding set of human values, is superior to any other. Consequently, pagan societies tend to become inegalitarian. . . . Might makes right and soon displaces the rule of law."[47]

Monotheism, on the other hand, Satinover points out, tends to be egalitarian, with everyone accountable to one Creator, who is distinct from His creatures and creation. Instincts are therefore not worshipped, but instead people worship the unchanging, just, and impartial Deity.[48]

Pagan values are dangerous enough in the lives of adults. Put them in the hands of emancipated youth, and there is truly the making of individual and collective disaster. Once the young pagans on the Facebook, MySpace, and Meetup Web sites form or join covens, we will have a whole new concept of teen street gangs, as they discover and harness the darkest forces in the universe to do the bidding of immature tastes, wishes, and values.

CHAPTER 6

Managing Pandora: What Can Parents Do?

"My daughter approached me today about doing a vision quest assignment. I am opting her out of this assignment. I do not want her participating in an animistic, spiritistic ceremony in order to receive a supernatural message from a spirit guide. Please give her an alternate assignment that reflects our family's biblical Christian worldview." (From an Ohio father's letter to his daughter's teacher)

It's difficult enough to raise children when our only concerns are the age-old matters of their health, safety, Sunday school training, career path, and marriage. To add the worry that they might be entrapped by deadly spiritual forces is almost too much. But the world we inhabit today calls for a new type of parenting.

There's great hope. Remember Who we have on our side.

Practically speaking, though, how do we navigate the dangers, short of locking each child in a room and saying, "Stay there, honey. You can come out when you're twenty-one"?

Roll Up Your Sleeves

Just like any other avenue of parenting, there's one bottom-line issue: it's hard work. And for those who like easy answers and quick fixes, the product (the child) will suffer. This is true in all aspects of parenting, but spiritual vigilance is needed more than ever, and that takes time, sweat, research, courage, and prayer.

To grow a bountiful crop, one must prepare the soil. So step one: the first plot of land is oneself. Huh? I have to work on *me* first? Well, of course. That's where it all starts.

Too many parents have called their pastors, friends, and counselors *after the fact* with horror stories that could have been prevented if the *parents themselves* had done some soul-searching and priority-checking early on. Then they might have known what they were dealing with and done the hard work needed ahead of time. We're always telling our kids to do their homework, but the same advice applies to us.

How can a parent know about spiritual danger and take precautions? How can parents develop that all-important quality of *spiritual discernment* on behalf of their children?

Preparing the Home Soil, Part 1

Here are the absolute first steps that a person must take.

1. **Know Christ as your Lord and Savior.** Does this need to be said? Perhaps it does, because some parents who have picked up this book may not be on solid ground with Jesus. If you have not confessed your own sins, repented, and asked Christ into your heart, perhaps now is the time to do that.

2. **Know what the Word of God says.** There's no better tutor on spiritual matters than the Bible. In Scripture you learn about the character of God, why Christ came, what He stands for, how humans relate to God, and the nature of the Holy Spirit versus the fallen angels of the spiritual world.

3. **Study and pray.** Read, and read again what Scripture says. Get involved in one or more Bible studies. Attend a Bible-based church regularly with your family. And daily set aside a private prayer time with God. God's work in your mind and heart will begin to make changes from the inside out, and you will develop the eyes and mind of discernment.

4. **Lead your child to Christ.** Make sure your child believes in Jesus Christ. This question needs to be directed personally and specifically (and also gently and happily) to your son or daughter at the appropriate age, once the salvation message of the gospel has been presented. It's not enough for a child to have attended classes at church or to have been through confirmation or another traditional group activity. Many kids leave Christianity because the whole process never got down to them personally. As the saying goes, God doesn't have grandchildren, just children. We are each responsible for making that faith decision ourselves.

Preparing the Home Soil, Part 2

So let's say you, your spouse, and your child are all Christians. Praise the Lord! So that's all there is to it, right?

Well, as you read earlier, not necessarily. Satan will mount fierce spiritual attacks against Christians to test their faith and throw trials and stumbling blocks in their paths, with the goal of drawing them away from Christ if possible, or to distract and discourage them so they fail to bring others to know the Lord. But do not be discouraged. There is tremendous hope.

You and your family will be ready if you *set up a framework* for your child that will minimize exposure to spiritual danger in the first place. Some background preparation will need to be done by you.

1. **Choose an educational climate that maximizes Christian faith and minimizes deception and danger.** It cannot be said strongly enough: *get your children out of the*

public schools and nonreligious private schools. The core philosophies, curricular materials, and permissive environments are hostile to Christianity and detrimental to strong character development. These institutions are also under the sway of unproven fads and special interest groups and often provide only a marginal education.

There's much more available on this subject, so we won't go into great depth here. But after bringing your child to Christ, this is the next most important thing you can do. Enroll your children in Christian schools or homeschool them. Children from these backgrounds are markedly different from public school children. They are happier, more secure, better educated, less aggressive, more hopeful in outlook, able to get along with people of all ages, and more sound in their faith.

2. **Limit television viewing and Internet use.** If you think this will be tough, you are correct. It will also mean a possible change of habits for you and your spouse. It will be absolutely worth it, though, because your kids will avoid adopting the vulgarity and spiritual misdirection of cultural habits and values.

As a result, you'll get a child who is more creative and resourceful, more settled in spirit, and less in need of constant, artificial stimulation. By all means, never allow children or teens to have their own televisions or Internet access in their rooms, away from parental supervision. Such access is a recipe for disaster.

One very positive alternative is to listen to Christian music in your home. Whether from your own CDs or a favorite FM station, there are some great tunes that will appeal to kids and penetrate their spirits in a God-honoring way.

3. **Get them involved in sound Christian youth activities.** I want to emphasize the term "sound" here, and this is where parents will need to do homework. Many great

youth groups exist, but there are also some that do little to build and strengthen a budding faith. Not that fun can't be part of youth activities, but too many youth groups don't offer much more than hay rides or field trips to concerts or video game parlors (a problem in itself). Others, as mentioned previously, dive into flagrantly un-Christian pursuits, such as meditation and other aspects of mysticism.

Ideally, a child might attend both a Sunday school class grounded in Scripture as well as a youth "bonding" group that builds on biblical knowledge. Occasional group activities such as service projects, field trips, and pizza parties are okay, as long as they are not the main focus.

4. **Encourage healthy friendships and discourage iffy ones.** As a parent, your instincts are usually right. If something about one of your child's friends makes you uncomfortable, trust your gut. Try to steer your child away early on, rather than waiting.

Your child's closest friends should not be self-avowed pagans, Wiccans, homosexuals, gender changers, or drug or alcohol users. Kids are drawn into shady activities and beliefs by peers. Children do not need to carry the burden of evangelizing the lost, except at armslength. The close-in work of bringing the lost to Him is the job of adults.

Believers are told not to be unequally yoked with unbelievers (2 Cor. 6:14). This does not mean kids can't be acquaintances with them and can't witness—quite the contrary, Christians are supposed to witness to the lost. Yet the believer's close friendships and relationships are to be with other believers.

There are special challenges when the pagan or bisexual is a relative. You and your spouse will need to make decisions about how a pagan uncle, for example, interacts with your kids. Openly pagan, homosexual, bisexual, adulterous, or cross-dressing relatives should not be invited into your home, in my opinion, and this needs to be explained to your relative and your children in advance of holidays or visits as tactfully and lovingly as possible. Just shutting the door suddenly in someone's face would be hurtful. Yet the standard of godly behavior needs to be upheld within the walls of the home. Not to do so is to invite all kinds of compromised situations into your midst, as your children are watching and learning.

Outings and visits by your children away from your home to the relative in question are also highly risky, unless you are present. If your whole family is invited to the wedding of your niece, for instance, whose brother is a Wiccan, well, of course, everyone should go and interact with him in that environment. But attending *his* wedding to another Wiccan with your kids is not a great idea.

Just Say No

My husband taught me many valuable lessons along the way about raising kids. One was that it's easier to say "no" up front than to deal with the damage later.

It takes eyes of discernment to foresee the kinds of damage that may result, and turning to Scripture is an invaluable tool. So books, music, and movies that are dark, steeped in pagan practices, graphic sexuality, or violence, should not be a big question mark for parents. Just say "no."

Remember, this culture is built on money and profit. Most of what is available to our kids is produced for that motive alone—not because of intrinsic noble benefits, but solely to sell, catering to America's unquenchable desire for entertainment. Yet there's really not a lot of priority on "entertainment" in Scripture, especially not the kinds that most people today embrace.

Kids are designed to play and explore. But it's important to guide them in that natural curiosity toward constructive, God-created options. Wholesome friends and relatives, everyday activities, and the beauty of the world can be their "toys." If we steer them toward these choices early on, instead of planting them in front of the television or plugging them into earphones, they will have a natural curiosity and wonder about daily routines, people, and nature. And when reading age arrives, put in front of them stories with wholesome, constructive, rational, and godly topics.

How do daisies grow? What are all the parts of a butterfly's wing? How can I build a doghouse, sew a skirt, or make a pizza? How can I learn to play the guitar? Kids can have positive interests that tap into the abundant resources all around them.

Sadly, some clueless parents will instead let their sons explore Borders or Barnes and Noble and come to the cash register with a book that opens as follows: "In the distance a wave of blood was building. Red, towering, topped with spitting heads of fire. On a vast plain, a mass of vampires waited."

So begins the book *Lord of the Shadows*, book eleven in the Cirque du Freak series popular with boys.

And we wonder why kids have nightmares, show signs of hyper-activity, or begin to be fascinated with the occult. Think about it: *there are many life-affirming subjects available.* Why allow images of death—which is really what the occult is all about—in front of our precious children?

Find within yourself your *top priority,* which as a Christian is to please and obey God. I often imagine the scenario as we stand before the Lord one day and our deeds are rolled out for examination. Even though we know Christ will stand with believers to make atonement for our sins—as He did at the cross—still, Scripture tells us the books will be opened and everything will be known (Rev. 20:12).

Somehow I don't think the Lord will chastise a parent, saying, "Now, I'm not happy that you didn't let your children explore their every interest. You prevented your daughter from watching *Charmed,* and you didn't let your son listen to Nine Inch Nails or have buddies who were pagans. You know, you should have just let them *go through their little phases* and not worried about it."

Parents need to think bigger and separate their vision from the current culture. Life doesn't begin and end here, and some "phases" kids are going through end up tragically as they reject Christ altogether, sometimes permanently. Most parents, when they search their hearts, realize they don't want to take that chance.

Yet overreacting can be counterproductive. For instance, what should a mother do if she suspects something is spiritually awry with her daughter and then discovers candles and spell books in her room? Although the danger is very real, screaming and locking the girl in her room would not be the best way to handle the situation.

I have a friend who discovered something similar. After abject prayer and crying out to the Lord in private, my friend and her husband calmed down, then talked with their daughter, showing her the problem by revealing what Scripture teaches. It is hard to remain cool, calm, and collected in these situations, but self-control is critically important.

A parent should ask the child to pray together. Some new restrictions then need to be placed on friendships, and the occult material tossed out, but only after a discussion so the child understands why. If the child's attendance in church or youth group has lapsed, these activities need to be reinstated as a routine. As long as your children live under your roof, they should honor your beliefs and live under the godly framework of your home. And it's important to reinforce to your son or daughter three reasons why:

- "I love you."
- "God loves you."
- "In our house, we love God, and we honor Him."

The Importance of Dad

The distraught phone calls and e-mails I get are more often from mothers than fathers. When moms contact me, somewhere in the conversation, I'll ask, "What does your husband think about this?" Virtually every time the answer goes something like this: "Well, my husband isn't as convicted about this as I am. He thinks our daughter (or son) is just going through a phase, and he remembers what he did when he was a teenager, and he's just not worried."

Many of our kids' problems would be solved tomorrow if dads were more concerned. The philosophy above breaks down when the following facts are taken into consideration:

1. **Today's dangers are worse than those of twenty or thirty years ago.** I'm not saying that pagan practices, drugs, and sexual issues were nonexistent in the past. But they are seriously heightened in every dimension. There were books on spells then; now they are available on kids' cell phones. There were a few witches then; now they are their teachers. There were a few kids having sex in middle school then; now bisexual Goths are having group oral sex parties at age thirteen.

The media's all-pervasive reach into kids' minds and hearts (to the extent that parents allow it) cannot be overestimated. We have *no idea* what kind of people we are producing in the Internet, Ipod, and cell-phone age. How bad can the damage be? We will find out in the future, but as it pertains to your child, don't assume that the past gives you any security. This is truly a different age. Barbarians, indeed, are in the making. Don't let one of them be your child.

2. **Today's parents were raised in a traditional culture; our kids are not.** Virtually all of us who are now adults were raised by parents who were more traditional than we are, and in an era when certain Christian norms were still assumed. Now, anti-Christian hostility and smashing moral and spiritual boundaries are becoming the norm. You can't simply turn your child loose in the world without some clear boundaries.

3. **How well did Dad turn out?** A laissez-faire attitude presupposes that "Dad" has turned out great. Upon objective examination, that may not hold up. Virtually everyone has some unwanted baggage, and the truly humble person will have regrets about the past. So if drugs were a part of your youth, and you struggled to overcome them, imagine your

child having both drugs *and* demonic influence to overcome. Everything you did, they will do *worse*. The end can
truly be horrifying as our kids' issues turn out to be much
more than a phase. You may have fathered an illegitimate
child; your daughter may bear three kids out of wedlock in
the commune with two Druid boyfriends. And some parents, especially fathers, think that kids need to be "tough-
ened up" to be ready to "face reality." Today's reality for
your child may mean friends who cut themselves and kids
who chant to goddesses at sleepovers. Is this *really* what
you want your child to face?

4. **Don't worry about so-called hypocrisy.** Many parents,
   especially fathers, have bought the idea that if you made a
   certain mistake when you were young, you have no
   grounds upon which to forbid that same action in your
   child's life. It's time to stop and think about how irrational
   this is. Why do parents teach children not to touch a hot
   stove? *Because we once touched one, and it hurt.* If our past experience, all of it, can't be used for our child's benefit, then
   we are pretty much useless to our kids.

5. **Dad is responsible to God for the caretaking of children.** Every father will have to stand before God and defend his fathering actions or nonactions because he is the
   head of the family God has given him. Think about this before shrugging at your son's "God is dead" tattoo.

The Choices That Remain

Is pretty much everything off limits, then? Not at all. We have abun-
dance in America of *everything*, and that includes a wealth of great options for kids. From Laura Ingalls Wilder books to Veggie Tales, there
are lots of wholesome and stimulating media out there for youth.

But the key to making wise decisions is to start when your children are young and to set up a Christian framework as described
above.

If you are reading this book and you have a rebellious teen, it's not a hopeless case by any means. Ground yourself in God's Word, pray constantly, and decide that no matter what, you will hang tough, and with love. Things could get a little challenging.

One parent I talked with some months ago told me about her seventeen-year-old son. Raised as a Christian, he began listening to dark "alternative" music recommended by a new group of friends. She had seen him change before her eyes, and she could sense the changes were spiritual. Surly and hostile, he became so angry at her one day while her husband was at work that she tearfully called the police. After spending a night in jail, though, her son seemed to have a changed attitude. His cellmates had given him a different perspective. One of them had scolded him: "You said *what* to yo' Mama? Boy, if I'd ever said that to my mama, she'd have whipped me good!" Sometimes God uses surprising messengers to open our eyes.

Practically speaking, though, what books, movies, and music *can* we feel comfortable allowing our kids? The approach is different with each child, depending on the child's personality. Some kids seem born with good sense and need only moderate guidance. Others are intrinsic risk-takers and may need your constant oversight.

Regarding non-Christian media choices, consider these factors:

- Overall tone: dark, depressing, gory, Christless, hopeless, or too sexualized
- Blatant disrespect toward God, biblical values, and Christians

Then, if the book or movie passes muster on these two fronts, consider one more test:

- Volume: how much importance/time does this non-Christian material take in your child's life and thoughts?

Using these guidelines, it's easy to reject much of modern youth music. Your son wants to listen to a band called Suicidal Tendencies? That's an easy "no." Ditto for bands with names that mock the Lord, as well as much of today's comedy, often openly blasphemous. Remember: "You shall love the Lord your God with all your heart, with all your soul, and with all your mind" (Matt. 22:37).

I would reject all of Philip Pullman's books, and I would reject all the Harry Potter books. Pullman's books are blatantly pagan and anti-Christian. Although intriguing, the plots are gloomy and hopeless, with adult themes children just don't need. The Potter books were immediately in my "no" pile because they feature children being tutored positively in witchcraft.

Some decisions, however, are less clear-cut, and if you want to protect your child's spiritual integrity, you'll have to do lots of pre-screening.

The Power of Prayer

How should you contend against the spiritual forces of darkness that would keep you and your children away from God? Scripture provides clear direction. Christ himself told his disciples that powerful faith, prayer, and fasting can overcome potent demonic forces (Matt. 17:21).

Constant prayer for your children is not simply an aid; it is your *responsibility* as parents. Fasting may need to be added to the daily habit of prayer in times of intense challenges. And lifelong Bible study is the foundation upon which all your actions should rest.

Sometimes Christians will say, "I'm waiting for God to tell me what to do." Although that can be the right course of action in some situations, often God will remain silent. It may be because *He has already told us in His Word.* He has already said that parents are to be the teachers and trainers of their children, that divination (fortune-telling) is wrong, and praying to anyone but Him is a violation of the first commandment.

The cherished gift of Scripture is an invaluable resource for parents going through the difficult days of parenting. And the answers are not always easy, the results not always immediate.

But in the darkest hours, remember that if you are faithful and obedient, the glorious fruit will, in His good time, ripen on the tree.

"Yet in all these things we are more than conquerors through Him who loved us. For I am persuaded that neither death nor life, nor angels nor principalities nor powers, nor things present nor things to come, nor height nor depth, nor any other created thing, shall

"Come to Me, all you who labor and are heavy laden, and I will give you rest" (Matt. 11:28).

be able to separate us from the love of God which is in Christ Jesus our Lord" (Rom. 8:37–39).

Notes

Chapter 1:
"Laying the Foundation to Build Young Pagans"

1. Compiled from information on "Top Twenty Religions in the U.S." on *http://www.adherents.com/rel_USA.html*. This figure combines the numbers of adult Wiccans/pagans, Unitarian Universalists, Spiritualists, and New Age adherents.
2. *http://www.CWIPP.org_, NewsCWIPP no. 3*, September 5, 2003, as well as e-mail communications between Dr. Peter Jones and the author.
3. McLaughlin and Brilliant, *Healing the Hate*, 64–66.
4. Convention on the Rights of the Child, United Nations General Assembly, Document A/RES/44/25 (12 December 1989) with Annex. Text of Declaration available at *http://www.unhchr.ch/html/menu3/b/k2crc.htm*.
5. *http://www.ncac.org/action_issues/Nudity_&_Pornography.cfm*.
6. *http://www.ncac.org/about/pos.cfm*.
7. Declaration of the Rights of the Child, Article 24.
8. "Study: Potter Readers More Occultic," *World Net Daily*, *http://www.worldnetdaily.com/news/article.asp?ARTICLE_ID=28124*, June 30, 2002.
9. Berneking and Joern, eds., *Re-Membering and Re-Imagining*, 59–60.
10. Davis, *Goddess Unmasked*, 28.
11. *http://www.mnchurches.org/pages/staff/chemberlinp.html*.
12. Berneking and Joern, eds., *Re-Membering and Re-Imagining*, 56–58.
13. *http://www.earthcharterinaction.org/2000/10/the_earth_charter.html*.
14. *http://www.pcusa.org/environment/earthday2005-godsearth-article.htm*.

15. Steichen, *Ungodly Rage: The Hidden Face of Catholic Feminism,* 74.

16. *http://www.hds.harvard.edu/wsrp/scholarship/rfmc/rfm_video .htm*

17. *http://www.hds.harvard.edu/news/article_archive/labyrinth.html.*

18. "VA Will Allow Wiccan Symbol on Gravestones," Dennis Camire, *USA Today* (April 24, 2007): 3A.

19. *http://newsweek.washingtonpost.com/onfaith/susan_brooks_thistle thwaite/2007/07/some_of_my_best_friends_are_wi.html.*

Chapter 2:
"Do What You Will: The Core Tenets of the New Spirituality"

1. Ewing, *The Becoming.*

2. The name of a "Jesus" or a "Christ" is often used by witches, as many are practicing within denominations of Christianity or have some Christian background. But these "Christs" as witches believe him to be, do not resemble the real person of Christ presented in Scripture. Christ, being One with the Trinitarian God from the beginning (Colossians, Ephesians) condemned witchcraft, and any witch who has knowledge about Christian doctrine would reject Him on this basis.

3. Starhawk, *Truth or Dare,* 24.

4. Adler, *Drawing Down the Moon,* 28.

5. Bowes, *Notions and Potions,* 78, 97.

6. Allen, "The Scholars and the Goddess," *http://www.theatlantic .com/issues/2001/01/allen.htm.*

7. Jones, *Gospel Truth/Pagan Lies,* 90.

8. Adler, *Drawing Down the Moon,* 20.

9. Jones, *Spirit Wars,* 178.

10. Starhawk, *The Spiral Dance,* 26–30.

11. Allen, "The Scholars and the Goddess."

12. Davis, *Goddess Unmasked,* 41–52.

13. Ibid., 54.

14. Davis, *Goddess Unmasked*, 53–83.
15. Ibid., 83–84.
16. Adler, *Drawing Down the Moon*, 162–65.
17. Edwards, "Wicca Infiltrates the Church," also at *http://www .ucmpage.org/articles/Wicca_story2.html.*
18. Newport, *The New Age Movement and the Biblical Worldview*, 225–26.
19. Artress, *Walking a Sacred Path*, 15.
20. Rain, *Spellcraft for Teens*, 46.
21. Gardner, *The Meaning of Witchcraft*, 9.
22. Adler, *Drawing Down the Moon*, 110, 125.
23. Starhawk, *The Spiral Dance*, 37.
24. Bowes, *Notions and Potions*, 14.
25. Hawkins, *Witchcraft: Exploring the World of Wicca*, 79–82.
26. Monaghan, *Wild Girls: The Path of the Young Goddess*, 128.
27. Ravenwolf, *Teen Witch*, 42–46 and Monaghan, *Wild Girls*, 45–47.
28. Ravenwolf, *Teen Witch*, 7–8.
29. Monaghan, *Wild Girls*, 202.
30. Ibid., 43–44.
31. Adler, *Drawing Down the Moon*, viii.
32. Artress, *Walking a Sacred Path*, 8.
33. Johnson, *She Who Is*, 26.
34. Gross, *Feminism & Religion*, 198.
35. Winter, et al., *Defecting in Place*, 159.
36. Steichen, *Ungodly Rage*, 71.
37. Cabot/Mills, *Celebrate the Earth*, 32.
38. Ravenwolf, *Teen Witch*, 8.
39. Monaghan, *Wild Girls*, 78.
40. Steichen, *Ungodly Rage*, 201–10.
41. Gross, *Feminism & Religion*, 228.
42. Starhawk, *The Spiral Dance*, 36, 38.
43. Walsch, *Conversations with God for Teens*, 85–86.
44. Buckland, *Witchcraft from the Inside*, 130.
45. Speech delivered by Hailson at Damaris Conference, Dallas, Texas, November 6, 1999, attended by the author.

46. Monaghan, *Wild Girls,* xv.
47. Ibid., 81.
48. Ibid., xv.
49. Starhawk, *The Spiral Dance,* 141.
50. Rowling, *Harry Potter and the Prisoner of Azkaban,* 28–30.
51. Berneking and Joern, eds., *Re-Membering and Re-Imagining,* 32.
52. Sanders, "Matthew Fox's Techno Cosmic Mass," *1, 4, 5, 8,* SCP Newsletter.

Chapter 3:
"The Spiritual Consequences of Paganism"

1. Newport, *The New Age Movement and the Biblical Worldview,* 576.
2. Ibid.
3. Lewis, C. S., *The Screwtape Letters,* Preface.
4. *http://www.acim.org.*
5. Hillstrom, *Testing the Spirits,* 25–26.
6. *http://www.johnedward.net/.*
7. Hillstrom, *Testing the Spirits,* 19.
8. Guadalupe Rosalez's personal account in *The Goddess Revival,* 200.
9. Ravenwolf, *Teen Witch.*

Chapter 4:
"Outreach: How, Why, and Where Paganism Connects with Kids"

1. That a fallen, sinful condition is the natural state of humans is a foundation of Christian doctrine, starting with the temptation and fall in the Garden of Eden (Genesis 3) and expressed in many other passages in Scripture. Some of the more familiar are Psalm 94:11, "The Lord knows the thoughts of man, that they are futile;" Jeremiah 17: 9, "The heart is deceitful above all things

and desperately wicked; Who can know it?" and Romans 3:23, " . . . for all have sinned and fall short of the glory of God."

2. *http://www.marketingcharts.com/interactive/teen-market-to-surpass-200-billion-by-2011-despite-population-decline-817/.*

3. *http://www.cbsnews.com/stories/2006/06/09/gentech/main 1698246.shtml.*

4. *http://news.bbc.co.uk/2/hi/entertainment/6912529.stm.*

5. Virtue, *The Care and Feeding of Indigo Children,* 34.

6. *http://cncpaganpride.org/2006/index.php/gallery_archives/home.*

7. *http://www.harmonytribe.org/shf2007/shf2007.html.*

8. *http://www.witchletsinthewoods.org.*

9. *http://www.geocities.com/RainForest/2111/personal.html.*

10. "Hello, Father, I'm a Witch," at *http://www.witchvox.com/va/dt_va. html?a=usct&c=teen&id=10988.*

11. From the blog of M. Macha Nightmare, *http://besom.blogspot.com/ 2006/10/back-from-paganistan.html.*

12. *http://www.llewellyn.com/history/event.php?id=187.*

13. *http://fremontartscouncil.org/events_seasonal.html.*

14. *http://www.seattle.gov/parks/proparks/projects/lincolnannex.htm.*

15. *http://www.spiralscouts.org.*

16. *http://www.fcps.edu/WestfieldHS/students/activities.htm.*

17. *http://www.vannuyshs.org/school_clubs_listing.jsp.*

18. As referenced at *http://www.religioustolerance.org/sch_clot5.htm.*

19. *http://www.witchvox.com/va/dt_va.html?a=usfl&c=cases&id=2351.*

20. For example, the PBS "Frontline" documentary, "Jefferson's Blood," May 2, 2000, dwelt on the relationship between Jefferson and Sally Hemings. Teacher's guides were available from PBS to accompany classroom instruction using this resource. At *http://www.pbs.org/wgbh/pages/frontline/shows/jefferson/.*

21. *http://www.nea.org/neatoday/0004/resource.html.*

22. *http://www.dpi.wi.gov/eis/observe.html#anchor18.*

23. "Pagan Christmas ritual pressed on young kids," *WorldNet Daily* News, December 8, 2006, *http://worldnetdaily.com/news/article.asp? ARTICLE_ID=53250.*

24. *Today Show,* June 5, 2003.

25. *http://www.timesonline.co.uk/tol/news/uk/education/article1600686.ece.*
26. Roach, *The Salem Witch Trials*, 308–9 and elsewhere throughout the book.
27. SciFi channel, "Evil," May 20, 2003, 10–11:00 p.m.
28. "The greening of the classroom: Do kids learn junk environmentalism in schools?" by Michael Chapman, *Investor's Business Daily* (September 29, 1998), as cited on *http://www.junkscience.com/sep98/learnjun.htm.*
29. "Amid Concerns, Bill Promotes 'Scientifically sound' environmentalism," *CNS News*, May 15, 2001, *http://www.CNSNews.com.*
30. Randal C. Archibold, "Court Review Sought in Bedford Paganism Suit," *New York Times*, June 30, 2001, *http://query.nytimes.com/gst/fullpage.html?res=9E0CE5D61539F933A05755C0A9679C8B63&n=Top/Reference/Times%20Topics/Subjects/R/Religion%20and%20Belief.*
31. "Colors of the Wind," lyrics by Stephen Schwartz, music by Alan Mencken, Copyright 1995, Hal Leonard Music.
32. *http://www.earthday.net/news/04-03-07_release.aspx.*
33. *http://www.academia.org/campus_reports/1998/november_1998_5.html.*
34. *http://afamichigan.org/index.php?p=29.*
35. Cart, ed., *Love & Sex: Ten Stories of Truth*, 45–57.
36. Block, *Dangerous Angels*, 210–11.
37. Ibid., 210–52.
38. Advertisement, *Columbus Alive* (January 6, 2000): 5.
39. *Upper Arlington* [Ohio] *News* (July 30, 2003): 9A.
40. *http://www.scholastic.com/harrypotter/community/archive/index.htm.*
41. *http://content.scholastic.com/browse/unitplan.jsp?id=284.*
42. *http://www.scholastic.com/titles/index.htm.*
43. *http://www.webenglishteacher.com/rowling.html.*
44. "The Lore of 'Harry Potter,'" *USA Today* (November 18, 2001): 1E–3E.
45. Ibid., 2E.
46. Phone conversations with the author.

47. Kraemer, Christine Hoff. "Pagans and Christians: Toward a Reconciliation of Opposites," *http://www.inhumandecency.org/christine/pagans.html.*
48. *http://www.cokesbury.com.*
49. *http://www.renewnetwork.org.*
50. *http://www.bridges-across.org/ba/lukash_jayelle.htm.*
51. *http://www.missionamerica.com/feminist.php?articlenum=2* on the writings of Winter. See also *Sojourners* magazine, July/August 1997.
52. *http://www.lighthousetrailsresearch.com/warrentwo.htm.*
53. "Which Witch of a Witch Am I?" *http://www.witchvox.com/va/dt_va.html?a=ussc&c=teen&id=11006.*
54. Wishart, *Teen Goddess,* 6–16.

Chapter 5:
"The Dangers of Living a Pagan Lifestyle"

1. Hillstrom, *Testing the Spirits,* 38.
2. Monaghan, *Wild Girls,* 108.
3. *http://www.bmezine.com/ritual/A40630/cltthequ.html.*
4. Rev. Steve Schlissel (Pastor, Messiah Congregation, Brooklyn, New York), "Body Modification: The Return to Paganism," *American Vision's Biblical Worldview* (October 1997): 4–8.
5. Ibid., 6.
6. Bernall, *She Said Yes,* 50.
7. *http://www.worldnetdaily.com/news/article.asp?ARTICLE_ID=40259, September 2, 2004.*
8. Ewing, *Goddess of the Night,* 55–59.
9. Block, *Girl Goddess # 9,* 103, 104.
10. *http://www.burningman.com/.*
11. Westerfeld, *Peeps,* 3, 22, 296.
12. *http://www.gurl.com/about/help/pages/0,,629823,00.html.*
13. Starhawk, "The Five Point Agenda," *http://www.reclaiming.org/about/directions/fivepoint-agenda.html.*

14. Starhawk, *Truth or Dare*, 25.
15. Ibid., 40–43.
16. Starhawk, *Truth or Dare*, 44–46.
17. Moore, *The Soul of Sex*, 8.
18. Ibid., 10–11.
19. Ibid., 41–43.
20. Ibid., 113.
21. Ibid., 63.
22. *http://www.neopagan.net/PaganPolyamory.html*.
23. As cited by Eller, *Living in the Lap of the Goddess*, 194.
24. Adler, *Drawing Down the Moon*, 340.
25. Davis, *Goddess Unmasked*, 339.
26. Adler, *Drawing Down the Moon*, 131.
27. "Rowling: Potter's Dumbledore Is Gay," Hillel Italie, October 20, 2007, *http://www.time.com/time/arts/article/0,8599,1674069,00.html?imw=Y*.
28. Satinover, *Homosexuality and the Politics of Truth*, 61.
29. Davis, *Goddess Unmasked*, 96.
30. Valentine, "Dragon Sense," in *The Duke Who Outlawed Jellybeans*.
31. *http://www.uua.org/obgltc/*.
32. For more details about how "GLBT" community youth centers operate, see *http://www.missionamerica.com/agenda.php?articlenum=47*.
33. Mitchell, *Tackling Gay Issues in School*, 78.
34. *http://www.wnd.com/news/article.asp?ARTICLE_ID=44306*.
35. For an example, see *http://www.critpath.org/pflag-talk/gid2.htm*.
36. "Homosexual Activist Group Teams Up With National PTA," *http://www.cnsnews.com/Nation/archive/200406/NAT20040624a.html*.
37. *http://www.nea.org/neatodayextra/safeschools.html*.
38. MacLaine, Shirley. *Going Within: A Guide for Inner Transformation* (Bantam, 1989), 197, as discussed by Jones and Brooke, *SCP Journal*, 10.
39. From a description by Anna Korn, Copyright 1988, on *http://www.cog.org/wicca/trads/faery.html*.

40. Sandfort et al., *Male Intergenerational Intimacy*, 267.

41. Jones and Brooke, "Strange Fire," 13.

42. Adler, *Drawing Down the Moon*, 344.

43. LaBarbera, Peter. "Turning Girls into Boys," *WorldNet Daily*, February 22, 2002, *http://www.worldnetdaily.com/news/article.asp? ARTICLE_ID=26569.*

44. Eller, *Living in the Lap of the Goddess*, 124.

45. Starhawk, *The Spiral Dance*, 106–7.

46. Hawkins, *Witchcraft: Exploring the World of Wicca*, 50.

47. Satinover, *Homosexuality and the Politics of Truth*, 232.

48. Ibid., 233–34.

Bibliography

Sources Favorable to Witchcraft/Feminist Spirituality/Neo-paganism—Nonfiction

Adler, Margot. *Drawing Down the Moon: Witches, Druids, Goddess-Worshippers and other Pagans in America Today.* New York: Penguin Compass, 1986.

Artress, Lauren. *Walking a Sacred Path: Rediscovering the Labyrinth as a Spiritual Practice,* Second edition. New York: Riverhead Books, 2006.

Berneking, Nancy J. and Joern, Pamela Carter, eds. *Re-Membering and Re-Imagining.* Cleveland: Pilgrim Press, 1995.

Bowes, Susan. *Notions and Potions: A Safe, Practical Guide to Creating Magic and Miracles.* New York: Sterling Publishing, 1997.

Buckland, Ray. *Witchcraft from the Inside.* St. Paul, MN: Llewellyn Publications, 1995.

Cabot, Laurie with Jean Mills. *Celebrate the Earth.* New York: Delta, 1994.

Camphausen, Rufus C. *Return of the Tribal: A Celebration of Body Adornment.* Rochester, Vermont: Park Street Press, 1997.

Eller, Cynthia. *Living in the Lap of the Goddess.* Boston: Beacon Press, 1995.

Gardner, Gerald. *The Meaning of Witchcraft.* York Beach, ME: Red Wheel/Weiser Books, 2004.

Gross, Rita. *Feminism & Religion.* Boston: Beacon Press, 1996.

Johnson, Elizabeth. *She Who Is: The Mystery of God in Feminist Theological Discourse.* New York: Crossroad, 1993.

Monaghan, Patricia. *Wild Girls: The Path of the Young Goddess.* St. Paul, MN: Llewellyn Publications, 2001.

Moore, Thomas. *The Soul of Sex: Cultivating Life as an Act of Love.* New York: HarperCollins Publishers, 1998.

Rain, Gwinevere. *Spellcasting for Teens: A Magical Guide to Writing and Casting Spells.* St. Paul, Minnesota: Llewellyn Publications, 2002.

Ravenwolf, Silver. *Teen Witch: Wicca for a New Generation.* St. Paul, Minnesota: Llewellyn Publications, 1999.

_____. *Witches' Night Out.* St. Paul, MN: Llewellyn Publications, 2000.

Starhawk. *The Spiral Dance: A Rebirth of the Ancient Religion of the Great Goddess.* St. Paul, Minnesota: HarperSanFrancisco, 1979.

_____. *Truth or Dare: Encounters with Power, Authority and Mystery.* San Francisco: Harper & Row Publishers, 1987.

_____. "The Five Point Agenda," *http://www.reclaiming.org/about/ directions/fivepoint-agenda.html.*

Virtue, Doreen, PhD. *The Care and Feeding of Indigo Children.* Carlsbad, CA: Hay House, Inc., 2001.

Walsch, Neale Donald. *Conversations with God for Teens.* Charlottesville, VA: Hampton Roads Publishing Co., 2001.

Winter, Miriam Therese; Lummis, Adair; and Stokes, Allison. *Defecting in Place: Women Claiming Responsibility for Their Own Spiritual Lives.* New York: Crossroad, 1995.

Wishart, Catherine. *Teen Goddess: How to Look, Love & Live Like a Goddess.* St. Paul, MN: Llewellyn Publications, 2003.

Websites on Paganism

www.witchvox.com

www.cog.org

www.teenwitch.com

www.spiralscouts.org

www.gURL.com

www.cokesbury.com

www.neopagan.net

www.circlesanctuary.org

www.ymsp.org

www.uua.org

www.bmezine.com (Warning: Graphic content)

www.dreamroads.com

www.witchletsinthewoods.org

www.mnchurches.org

www.earthcharter.org

www.johnedward.net

www.llewellyn.com

www.religioustolerance.org

www.hds.harvard.edu

www.acim.org

www.paganpride.org

www.harmonytribe.org

www.bridges-across.org

www.inhumandecency.org

www.reclaiming.org

Sources Critical of Witchcraft/Feminist Spirituality/Neo-paganism—Nonfiction

Allen, Charlotte. "The Scholars and the Goddess." *Atlantic Monthly* (January 2001); *http://www.theatlantic.com/issues/2001/01/allen.htm*

Davis, Philip G. *Goddess Unmasked: The Rise of Neopagan Feminist Spirituality.* Dallas: Spence Publishing Company, 1998.

Edwards, Catherine. "Wicca Infiltrates the Church." *Insight Magazine,* vol. 15, no. 45 (December 6, 1999); *http://www.ucmpage.org/articles/wicca_story2.html*

Hawkins, Craig. *Witchcraft: Exploring the World of Wicca.* Grand Rapids, MI: Baker Books, 1996.

Hillstrom, Elizabeth. *Testing the Spirits.* Downers Grove, IL: InterVarsity Press, 1995.

Jones, Peter, PhD. *Gospel Truth/Pagan Lies.* Escondido, CA: Main Entry Editions, 1999.

————. *Spirit Wars: Pagan Revival in Christian America*. Escondido, CA: Main Entry Editions, 1997.

————, and Brooke, Tal. "Strange Fire: The Invasion of Pagan Sexuality." *SCP Journal*, volume 25:4–26:1 (2002): 4–14.

Lewis, C. S. *The Screwtape Letters* and *Screwtape Proposes a Toast*. New York: Macmillan Publishing Company, 1961. (Preface, Magdalen College, July 5, 1941).

Newport, John P. *The New Age Movement and the Biblical Worldview*. Grand Rapids, MI: Williams B. Eerdmans Publishing Company, 1998.

Sanders, Catherine. "Matthew Fox's Techno Cosmic Mass." *SCP Newsletter*, Spiritual Counterfeits Project (Spring 2002): 1, 4, 5, 8.

Satinover, Jeffrey, MD. *Homosexuality and the Politics of Truth*. Grand Rapids, MI: Baker Books, 1996.

SCP *Journal* and Newsletter, published by Spiritual Counterfeits Project, Editor: Tal Brooke, Berkeley, CA.

Spencer, Aida Besancon; Hailson, Donna F. G.; Kroeger, Catherine Clark; and Spencer, William David. *The Goddess Revival*. Grand Rapids, MI: Baker Books, 1995.

Steichen, Donna. *Ungodly Rage: The Hidden Face of Catholic Feminism*. San Francisco: Ignatius Press, 1991.

Helpful Websites

www.missionamerica.com
www.CWIPP.org
www.worldnetdaily.com
www.CNSNews.com
www.lighthousetrailsresearch.org
www.scp-inc.org
www.ucmpage.org
www.afamichigan.org
www.academia.org
www.renewnetwork.org

Youth Fiction

Antieau, Kim. *Mercy, Unbound.* New York: Simon Pulse, 2006.

Applegate, K. A. *Animorphs: The Sickness.* New York: Scholastic, Inc., 1999.

Bird, Isobel. *So Mote It Be,* Circle of Three series. New York: Avon Books, HarperCollins Publishers, 2001.

Block, Francesca Lia. *Dangerous Angels: the Weetzie Bat Books.* New York: HarperCollins Publishers, 1998.

_____. *Girl Goddess #9.* New York: HarperTrophy, 1996.

Cart, Michael, ed. *Love & Sex: Ten Stories of Truth.* New York: Simon & Schuster Books for Young Readers, 2001.

Ewing, Lynne. *Goddess of the Night,* Daughter of the Moon series for teens. New York: Hyperion Books for Children, 2000.

_____. *The Becoming.* New York: Hyperion, 2004.

Gilmour, H. B. and Reisfeld, Randi. *Kindred Spirits.* T'Witches series. New York: Scholastic, Inc., 2003.

Larbalestier, Justine. *Magic or Madness.* London: Firebird/Razorbill, Penguin Books, Ltd., 2005.

Levy, Stuart J. and Takeuchi, Naoko. *Sailor Moon: A Scout is Born.* Los Angeles and Tokyo: TokyoPop, 1999.

Nix, Garth. *Abhorsen.* New York: HarperCollins, 2003.

Petry, Ann. *Tituba of Salem Village.* New York: Harper Collins, 1991.

Pierce, Tamora. *Shatterglass,* no. 4 in The Circle Opens series. New York: Scholastic, Inc., 2003.

Pullman, Philip. *The Golden Compass.* New York: Alfred A. Knopf, 1995.

_____. *The Amber Spyglass.* New York: Dell-Yearling, 2000.

Rowling, J. K. *Harry Potter and the Sorcerer's Stone.* New York: Scholastic, Inc., 1997.

_____. *Harry Potter and the Prisoner of Azkaban.* New York: Scholastic Press, 1999.

_____. *Harry Potter and the Goblet of Fire.* New York: Scholastic Press, 2000.

_____. *Harry Potter and the Half-Blood Prince.* New York: Arthur A. Irvine Books, Scholastic, Inc., 2005.

Shan, Darren. *Cirque du Freak: Lord of the Shadows.* New York: Little Brown and Company, 2004.

Stroud, Jonathan. *The Golem's Eye.* New York: Miramax Books, Hyperion Books for Children, 2004.

Valentine, Johnny. *The Duke Who Outlawed Jellybeans.* Los Angeles: Alyson Wonderland, 1991.

Westerfield, Scott. *Peeps.* London: RazorBill, The Penguin Group, 2005.

www.scholastic.com

Other Sources

Bernall, Misty. *She Said Yes.* Farmington, PA, Plough Publishing House, 1999.

Convention on the Rights of the Child, United Nations General Assembly, Document A/RES/44/25 (December 12, 1989) with Annex. Text of Declaration available at *http://www.unhchr.ch/html/menu3/b/k2crc.htm*

McLaughlin, Karen A. and Brilliant, Kelly J. *Healing the Hate: A National Bias Crime Prevention Curriculum for Middle Schools.* Educational Development Center, Inc. Office of Juvenile Justice and Delinquency Prevention, U.S. Department of Justice, 1997.

Mitchell, Leif, ed. *Tackling Gay Issues in School*: A Resource Module, cosponsored by GLSEN (Gay, Lesbian and Straight Education Network), Planned Parenthood of Connecticut, 1999.

Roach, Marilynne K. *The Salem Witch Trials: A Day-by-Day Chronicle of a Community Under Siege.* New York: Cooper Square Press, 2002.

Sandfort, Theo, PhD; Brongersma, Edward, JD, van Naerssen, Alex, PhD, eds., *Male Intergenerational Intimacy.* Binghamton, NY: The Haworth Press, 1991.

The Today Show, New York, National Broadcasting Network.

World magazine, Asheville, NC.

Additional Informative Websites

www.pcusa.org
www.ncac.org
www.nea.org
www.bbc.co.uk
www.bridges-across.org
www.webenglishteacher.com
www.fcps.edu
www.vannuyshs.org
www.junkscience.com
www.libraryjournal.com
www.pbs.org
www.dpi.wi
www.timesonline.co.uk
www.earthday.net
www.time.com
www.cbsnews.com
www.adherents.com
www.newsweek.washingtonpost.com
www.marketingcharts.org
www.seattle.gov
www.fremontartscouncil.org